Jordanian–Israeli Relations
The peacebuilding experience

Jordan's peace treaty with Israel was unique as it bore the promise of what was termed a 'warm' peace between the two warring countries. With legitimacy provided by Madrid and Oslo, hopes for 'true' peace, as the Israelis would describe it, were high. This book explores the Jordanian–Israeli relations from a Jordanian perspective, focusing on the peacebuilding experience since 1994. In examining the reasons why a warm peace has not developed, the book focuses on the interplay between agency and structure on the Jordanian side, in relation to the Israeli–Palestinian context. In doing so, the book discusses the role of the various Jordanian leadership layers in the process and brings to light the intra-societal dynamics and particularities of the Jordanian social construct.

With research based on the premise that international relations are social constructions, meaning that facts are theory-laden and contexts matter to political actors since they influence their understanding of conflict and impact upon their decisions, the book also serves as an example of the application of an inter-disciplinary approach to analysing conflicts and subsequent peacebuilding experiences.

This book will be of interest to students of Politics and International Relations, History, Middle Eastern Studies and Social Studies, in particular those interested in the areas of Conflict Resolution and Peacebuilding.

Dr Mutayyam al O'ran holds a PhD in international conflict analysis and international relations from the University of Kent, UK. Her areas of expertise include international relations, conflict resolution/transformation and peacebuilding, in addition to Arab–Israeli relations and politics. Dr al O'ran is a member of the British Society for Middle Eastern Studies and she has published a number of articles in academic journals.

Routledge Studies in Middle Eastern Politics

Algeria in Transition
Reforms and development prospects
Ahmed Aghrout with Redha M. Bougherira

Palestinian Refugee Repatriation
Global perspectives
Edited by Michael Dumper

The International Politics of the Persian Gulf
A cultural genealogy
Arshin Adib-Moghaddam

Israeli Politics and the First Palestinian Intifada
Political opportunities, framing processes and contentious politics
Eitan Y. Alimi

Democratization in Morocco
The political elite and struggles for power in the post-independence state
Lise Storm

Secular and Islamic Politics in Turkey
The making of the justice and development party
Ümit Cizre

The United States and Iran
Sanctions, wars and the policy of dual containment
Sasan Fayazmanesh

Civil Society in Algeria
The political functions of associational life
Andrea Liverani

Jordanian–Israeli Relations
The peacebuilding experience
Mutayyam al O'ran

Jordanian–Israeli Relations

The peacebuilding experience

Mutayyam al O'ran

Routledge
Taylor & Francis Group

LONDON AND NEW YORK

Transferred to digital printing 2010
First published 2009
by Routledge
2 Park Square, Milton Park, Abingdon, Oxon OX14 4RN

Simultaneously published in the USA and Canada
by Routledge
270 Madison Ave, New York, NY 10016

Routledge is an imprint of the Taylor & Francis Group, an informa business

© 2009 Mutayyam al O'ran

Typeset in Times New Roman by
Bookcraft Ltd, Gloucestershire

British Library Cataloguing in Publication Data
A catalogue record for this book is available from the British Library

Library of Congress Cataloging in Publication Data
Al O'ran, Mutayyam, 1972–
Jordanian–Israeli relations: the peacebuilding experience, Mutayyam
al O'ran
  p.cm.
  Includes bibliographical references and index.
  1. Jordan—Foreign relations—Israel. 2. Israel—Foreign relations
  —Jordan. 3. Arab–Israeli conflict—1993—Peace. 4. Jordan—Politics
  and government—1999. 5. Israel–Politics and government—1993–
  I. Title.
DS154.16.I75A4 2008
327.569505694–dc22   2008023420

ISBN13: 978-0-415-43784-4 (hbk)
ISBN13: 978-0-415-61278-4 (pbk)
ISBN13: 978-0-203-88692-2 (ebk)

ISBN10: 0-415-43784-9 (hbk)
ISBN10: 0-415-61278-0 (pbk)
ISBN10: 0-203-88692-5 (ebk)

I dedicate this work to the ones whose ideals put me on the path of peace research and without whose support, love and encouragement, this humble effort would never have seen the light of day. More specifically, I dedicate it to my beloved mother, Muna al O'ran, to my precious Maysa and dearest Manal and Mudar. Thank you for being my family and friends. I also dedicate this book to the memory of my father, Suleiman al O'ran.

Contents

Acknowledgements   ix
Preface   xi
Abbreviations   xiii

1   Introduction   1

2   The long journey to peace   9

3   Achieving and building peace (1994–2003)   31

4   Obstacles to a warm peace at the structural level   49

5   The refugee question and peace   67

6   Leaderships and the peacebuilding process   73

7   The road to a warm peace   83

Notes   89
Bibliography   97
Index   109

Acknowledgements

This work has benefited from the valuable assistance and advice of a number of individuals in Jordan and Britain. In Jordan, I am thankful to all who accorded me interviews at various stages of my work and despite their hectic schedules and constant travel, especially their Excellencies Mr Marwan Muasher, Gen. Ali Shukri and Adnan Abu Odeh. I am grateful to the staff at the *Centre d'Etudes et Recherches du Moyen Orient* in Amman for placing the resources of their library at my disposal. Similarly, I thank the staff at Jordan University Archives and the Royal Scientific Society for granting me access to their publications. I am also particularly grateful to the Global Research in International Affairs (GLORIA) Centre for allowing me full use of an article I published in the December 2006 issue of the *Middle East Review of International Affairs* Journal. Distinguished scholars whose unpublished academic works (including doctoral theses) were made available to me to benefit from, deserve my special thanks and appreciation, especially Dr Adiba Mango.

I also extend my deepest appreciation and sincere gratitude to Professors Hugh Miall and Gerd Nonneman and Dr Neil Quilliam for their invaluable insights, support and encouragement, and above all, friendship.

As much as everybody's valuable insight and comments helped guide the research and enriched the analytical process, the failings and shortcomings of the work remain solely and entirely my own.

Preface

My keen interest in peacebuilding, conflict resolution in general and the Israeli–Arab conflict in particular is not merely attributed to all these being my areas of academic specialization, but also to my being a woman living in a turbulent region during continuously challenging times, a region known to the world as the Middle East. With conflicts raging in numerous Middle Eastern hot spots and, at times, outliving entire generations that witnessed their beginnings, one is met with sheer cynicism when broaching the topic of regional peace, let alone prospects of a warm Arab–Israeli one. Notwithstanding the frustrations breeding this cynicism, this last one is inadmissible. This is simply because the best time to contemplate peace is during ongoing violent conflict. Peace is what we struggle with our opponents to achieve. It requires stamina, unshaken faith and heroic sacrifices. It is certainly not an abstract notion that we are meant to praise in quiet conversation with trusted friends. Peace is made with people one fears and calls enemies, and the struggle to build it is even harder. Therefore, it is as timely as ever to talk of peace in the Middle East and to contemplate a warm one, more so because of the ongoing clashes, occupation, violence and deeply rooted frustrations.

In writing this book, I built on the premise that one of the most urgent and worthy prospects to pursue would be peace in the Middle East. This book is but a humble effort to examine the Jordanian–Israeli story of war and peace, a story worth telling not merely because of its relative obscurity (as testified by the dearth of academic literature on the topic), rather because the Jordanian–Israeli peace-building experience was meant to be a model of warm Arab–Israeli relations. It was intended to encapsulate a dream that, history confirms, only brave leaders contemplate; men and women determined to go down in history as veritable peacemakers who paid more than lip service to the cause.

However, the dream did not materialize in full and this book tries to explain why. In doing so, the book will focus on the Jordanian side and perspective, these being the least known and perhaps more relevant from a conflict resolution theory point of view. In understanding the Jordanian peace experience, valuable lessons could be learned about peacebuilding in general and within an Arab–Israeli context in particular, knowledge that could provide lenses through which other Arab–Israeli peace processes can be looked at and examined. Indeed, if the reader emerges with an idea of the kind of structural and agency-related challenges to anticipate in making and building peace, the book will have served its purpose in full.

Abbreviations

BATNA	Best Alternative to a Negotiated Agreement
IAF	Islamic Action Front
IMF	International Monetary Fund
MENA	Middle East and North Africa
PLO	Palestine Liberation Organization
PNA	Palestinian National Authority
QIZ	Qualified Industrial Zone
UNRWA	United Nations Relief and Works Agency
UNSCR	United Nations Security Council Resolution

1 Introduction

On 25 July 1994, Jordan and Israel signed the Washington Declaration, which ended the official state of belligerence between them since the foundation of the State of Israel in 1948. Three months later, a full-fledged peace treaty was signed between representatives of both countries in the Arava valley in the south of Jordan. The ceremony was attended by world leaders and key figures whose hopes for peace in the region were high and, seemingly at the time, well-founded. It seemed that the Arab–Israeli conflict was ending at last, having reached a hurtful stalemate that made a peaceful resolution to the conflict the only viable option. Jordan was the second Arab state, after Egypt, to sign a peace treaty with Israel; but in many ways, the treaty was unique. Peace with Egypt was concluded under the pressure of renewed hostilities, snatched from the teeth of opposition from other Arab countries in a world dominated by the cold war. Consequently, security arrangements in Sinai were at the centre of this peace treaty, with normalization serving as a bargaining card for the Egyptians. Peace with Jordan, on the other hand, was concluded after years of quiet dialogue and tacit understandings, with legitimacy provided by Madrid and Oslo, and in a world whose beacons were globalization, interdependence and the market. Accordingly, as Shimon Shamir pointed out, the treaty said little about security and a great deal about economic cooperation (Shlaim 2001: 544). Above all, it bore the seeds of a warm peace. Articles 5, 6 and 10 of the Jordan–Israel treaty of peace make explicit reference to normalization in the diplomatic, economic, cultural and scientific spheres. This was not only a treaty that set out obligations and rights, but it also provided a blueprint for complete normalization along all levels and in all spheres.

This book will explore why a 'warm peace' following the Israeli–Jordanian peace treaty of 1994 did not materialize, with warm peace understood as full normalization of relations at the political, economic and social levels enabling easy transfer and flow of people, goods and ideas. It will examine the continuing obstacles to such a peace, focusing primarily on the interplay between agency and structure on the Jordanian side, albeit in relation to the Israeli–Palestinian context. It also intends to examine the role of the various Jordanian leaderships in the process; a process that would bring to light the intra-societal dynamics and particularities of the Jordanian social construct. The aim of the study is to identify the key obstacles to a warm peace at the levels of agency and structure in Jordan, the assumption being that addressing them can help Jordanian–Israeli relations move forward and, hopefully, play a part in contributing to a comprehensive and lasting peace in the region.

One must confess that given the impact the Palestinian–Israeli conflict had on Jordan's demographic, social and political landscapes,[1] there was always doubt whether the conflict could be subjected to academic scrutiny from a non-Palestinian perspective. Those who argue against the feasibility of an independent Jordanian track and perspective mostly do so because the largest number of Palestinian refugees (estimated as per UNRWA statistics at 42 per cent of Palestinian refugees worldwide) resides in Jordan. However, this argument overlooks the fact that it never turned the country into a mere extension of the Occupied Territories; if anything, it was crucial in helping a distinct sense of Jordanian nationalism to emerge. Thus, it would be misleading to assume that a Jordanian perspective, especially at state-level, is identical to or simply secondary to a Palestinian one. Moreover, the disengagement between the East and West Banks on 31 July 1988 meant that Jordan no longer had claims to major territories occupied by Israel, which mainly reduced the issues under contention between the two states to some territorial claims and water rights.[2] Consequently, Jordan's ambitions based on the peace process differed from those of the PLO. Jordan mainly sought an end to its isolation following the Iraqi–Kuwaiti crisis, certain territorial demands and water rights, an end to the substitute homeland threat and economic dividends that would make the peace with Israel more acceptable domestically[3] given the conflict's bitter history and ensuing dehumanization of the enemy in the mainstream Arab political culture, not to mention the large number of citizens of Palestinian origin[4] living inside and outside camps.

The book tries to answer four questions: What are the obstacles to a 'warm peace' in the Jordanian–Israeli relationship from a Jordanian point of view? What is the role of leadership in peacebuilding, with specific reference to the case of Jordan? Are the Jordanian–Israeli peace treaty and peacebuilding process an elite deal or a broadly based reconciliation between societies? Taking account of the obstacles to a warm peace in Jordan, what do decision makers and informed observers believe should be the sequence of steps taken towards establishing a warmer peace in the Jordanian–Israeli relations?

The period covered by the book is one of the most crucial decades in modern Jordanian history, one in which Jordan transitioned from a state of war to a state of peace and from one monarch to another. However, the dearth of academic literature on this crucial period was not the only reason behind its selection, but rather the choice was guided by the theories of peacebuilding and reconciliation (a prerequisite for a 'warm peace') which speak of time frames of decades and generations. Therefore, the period from 1994 until 2003 was chosen, being the first decade after the peace treaty.

Who wanted peace?

In August of 1994, the Centre for Strategic Studies at Jordan University conducted a public poll (poll number 4), the objective of which was to measure support within the Jordanian public for the Jordanian–Israeli peace negotiations following the Washington Declaration signed between the two countries. The national sample covering all segments of society and sectors indicated that 80.2 per cent of the respondents supported Jordan's signing of the Washington Declaration while 14.1 per cent opposed it; of the various reasons given for the opposition, religious ones were the most common. Of the total number of respondents, 71.2 per cent said they expected Jordan to regain its full territorial rights, while 75.9 per cent of them thought it would also regain all its water rights and a majority of 82.8 per cent expected the economic situation to improve. Obviously, the general Jordanian mood was pro-peace, especially since the party most directly concerned, the Palestinians, signed a declaration of principles with Israel by which both parties ended the state of belligerence between them. The declaration presumably brought to a near-end the conflict that officially started in the first decades of the twentieth century and, more importantly, removed all compelling reasons why other Arab states should not seek peace with Israel.

Indeed, given the international and regional developments in the wake of the Second Gulf War and the economic crises they meant for Jordan, peace was becoming more a pragmatic necessity than the result of a paradigm shift as far as the people were concerned. In addition to welcome economic improvements, East Bank Jordanians hoped that peace would put an end to the threat of Jordan becoming a substitute homeland for the stateless Palestinians. Moreover, King Hussein hailed the peace as a key strategic accomplishment that would curb the eastern expansion of the Jewish state itself.

As to the Palestinian refugees in particular, they were mostly eager for the process to move forward as it meant an approaching end to their dilemma, and since a two-state concept is fundamentally incompatible with the right of return of all refugees, it was widely understood the solution would most likely take monetary form. Initially, the declaration of principles between PLO and Israel was a blow to the refugee community as it meant that their own leadership had subordinated the right of return – considered the pillar of faith of the Palestinian struggle – for its own wishes, namely the establishment of a state. However, with Jordan signing a peace treaty, the overall mood changed into an optimistic one, signalling a close resolution to all pending issues.[5]

What kind of peace?

So Jordan was in favour of peace – but what kind of peace? The meaning of peace is important. Peace meant not so much an end to the state of belligerence between the two states since there had been more or less a de facto peace since 1967 (albeit interrupted by al-Karameh events in 1968), but rather an end to the threat of a possible invasion, an eastward expansion that would be unstoppable (especially in the absence of a Soviet super-power and a defeated Iraqi military). Peace would mean an economic dividend that could be felt by the average person.

Despite the overwhelming support for peace, the type of peace envisaged by the public was formal, not warm. For those East Bank citizens not ideologically opposed to normalization of relations with Israel, a favourable change to the structure of the relationship between their developing, sovereignty-threatened, resource-poor country and Israel (the regional economic and military superpower) was necessary to foster new cognitive beliefs that would make contemplating a warmer peace possible given the existing psychological baggage that decades of violence and hostility have caused. Full normalization for the Palestinian refugees in Jordan (to those not ideologically opposed to it) was indeed premature to discuss as it depended upon progress along the Palestinian–Israeli track for reasons of loyalty and direct dependence on outcome particularly concerning the refugee question.

The potential of warm peace existed with the majority of citizens from both communities not ideologically opposed to peace with Israel (seemingly a majority judging by the pro-peace public poll) and the crux of this book is to explain why it failed to materialize.

The meaning of peacebuilding

Given the academic nature of this work, defining key terminology is of the essence to prevent confusion or reliance on less than accurate mainstream interpretations. A term that is of particular significance to this work is 'peacebuilding'. According to Johan Galtung (1975), once a conflict is manifest, its resolution usually proceeds through stages identified as peacekeeping, peacemaking and peacebuilding.[6] Peacekeeping refers to the stage where the goal is to reduce the manifest violence through military intervention if necessary, while peacemaking refers to the process 'directed at reconciling political and strategic attitudes through mediation, negotiation, arbitration and conciliation' mainly at the top-level leadership (ibid.: 282). However, Galtung's definition of peacebuilding as addressing 'the practical implementation of peaceful social change through socio-economic reconstruction and development' (1975: 304) is incomplete because he overlooks a key factor in deep-rooted conflicts: the relational aspect. Ryan recognized this oversight from Galtung and emphasized the need to include the sociopsychological dimension into the equation otherwise all forms of restructuring would be in jeopardy (Miall *et al.* 1999). Therefore, the definition of peacebuilding advanced by this work is that it is *the actual implementation of agreements reached through economic and political restructuring processes in tandem with activities targeting the redefinition of the relationships between the protagonist parties along all levels of society; it is the interaction of agency and structure in a process headed towards full normalization, sustainable peace and reconciliation.* Perhaps a better way of explaining the definition further is clarifying that which it is not, and no better case to use than the Berlin Conference on peacebuilding, which defined the process as follows:

> Peacebuilding is ... in the first place a political undertaking, and not a developmental or humanitarian one; secondly, its priority is not the ending of conflict as such, but to prevent the resumption of violence; thirdly, the time dimension of post-conflict peacebuilding is short and medium term, whereas development and nation-building is long-term
>
> (Haugerudbraaten 1998)

Aside from the use of the oxymoron 'post-conflict peacebuilding' – since conflicts do not end with the halting of violence – the definition is, as far as this author is concerned, flawed. It reduces the process to maintaining a *settlement*, and as such confines the task of building peace to the political arena only, since it presumably has the authority and power to impose one. Surprisingly enough, the definition indicates a sharp contrast between peace and development, when prominent scholars (e.g. Azar, Galtung and Curle) perceive positive peace as development in its truest and broadest sense: development of human beings, their potential and environment. The temporal aspects of the process are also misrepresented, described as short- to mid-term only, contradicting the notion of *sustained* cooperative work to maintain the peace and what Boutros Ghali, in the supplement to the peace agenda, labelled as 'the creation of structures for the institutionalization of peace' (Cousens *et al.* 2001). This notion of sustainability is what prompted Lederach (1997) to set time frames for the various intervention options required for targeting peacebuilding.[7] Placing a plaster on a conflict situation through settlement is not the equivalent of tackling its root causes, and as such cannot be a guarantee against the recurrence of violence.

The author proposes a model for the study of peacebuilding following violent and deep-rooted conflict (like the Jordanian–Israeli one) in which focus falls simultaneously on structures and agency factors of relevance. Sociopolitics and economics become the primary foci for structure, while the study of agency, in Jordan's case, brings to the forefront the dominant cognitive and ideological beliefs of the agent groups most directly involved. This provides a better understanding of the conflict, its history, development and peacebuilding process. The model provides a point of reference that connects the past to the present while allowing for a projection into the future.

Not only is the Jordanian–Israeli conflict deep-rooted, but it is also asymmetric. Symmetric conflicts are between similar or relatively similar parties who have a conflict over issues such as land, resources or interests. Such conflicts tend to be amenable to straightforward resolution if the source of conflict is indeed an issue such as the one defined by the parties: objective, quantifiable or divisible. However, if the 'issues' pertain to the structure of the relationship between the parties, then they are asymmetric conflicts where interests are not the only problem but the very structure of the relationship (e.g. oppressor and oppressed, occupier and occupied, etc.) as well as factors that sustain the asymmetry. These can be existing *structures* (including the political culture) as well as unfavourable cognitive and ideological beliefs, hence the attention awarded to these factors by this book which uses them when analysing the conflict and examining the subsequent peacebuilding process. From a Jordanian point of view, the conflict with Israel is understood to be asymmetric, characterized by a relationship of dominance, a situation that is generally believed to have remained intact after peace. It is a result of the demonstrable tangible asymmetry of power-relations between both countries that Israel was able to safeguard its economic interests in the Occupied Territories over Jordan's. This is atop existing structures on the ground serving as constant reminders to Jordanians of the asymmetry. One particular example is the refugee camps in Jordan , which symbolize Israeli imposition on the political, social and demographic scene in Jordan. Therefore, notwithstanding a treaty of peace that legally safeguards Jordanian state sovereignty and, at least on paper, recognizes Jordan as an equal, the Jordanian perception of a persisting Israeli threat to identity and state survival lingers on, seemingly with good reason. Consequently, this perception cannot be overlooked when analysing the conflict or subsequent peacebuilding, hence the significance given by this book to explaining its history and development.

Conflict resolution and transformation theories

Just as *realism* emerged in reaction to political idealism, conflict resolution emerged as an alternative to the power-political framework (Aggestam 1999). It became a field of research in the 1950s and 1960s when a group of pioneer researchers from various disciplines, appalled by the mounting threat of the cold war and development of nuclear weapons, decided to study conflicts in general, applying knowledge from various fields to interpersonal, inter-group and international conflicts (Miall *et al.* 1999). To this day, this field of study remains one that encourages triangulation between the various disciplines in the pursuit of better understanding of conflicts, not with the purpose of eliminating them but rather constructively managing them. As such, the opposite of peace is not conflict but *violence*. Indeed, conflict resolution holds that conflict is an integral part of human society that can be a positive driving force for change and development.

Conflict resolution, as a new field of study, was initially unable to win support from adherents to the more well-established fields of international relations and politics. However, with the rise in number of conflicts of a nature unfamiliar to the school of international relations – such as conflicts around issues of ethnicity and breakdown of state structures and societies – attention shifted to conflict resolution scholars since they had the better knowledge of these less-examined variables. By shedding light on obscure causes for conflict, conflicts were presented in broader and more complex terms than a mere struggle between competing centres of power. Needs and sociopsychological considerations were part of the equation. Unlike realists, conflict-resolution advocates do not stop at achieving formal peace. The *sustainability* of peace by those directly affected by the conflict is a key requirement and measure for success. Conflict resolution makes a direct link between suppression of basic human needs and conflict, arguing that in order to resolve conflicts, the very relationship between the protagonists would have to be reconfigured in a manner that would sensitize the parties to their mutual needs. As such, a problem-solving approach is encouraged whereby an impartial mediator aids parties in communicating their true needs and building a working relationship that can help them achieve a mutually satisfying resolution.

Nevertheless, conflict resolution is weakened by its neglect of culture, power structures, power relations and relevant institutions, resulting in a linear, non-structural view of conflict that is not necessarily in line with its social realities. Conflict *transformation* theory finds more resonance among scholars and analysts since it stresses the importance of *structures* as causes for conflict. Structural violence, equality and justice are key concepts to the approach that emphasizes *positive peace* (Galtung 2001). The power asymmetry between the Palestinians and Israelis, for example, was reason for delayed positive action on the peace front. Until the Intifada of 1987, the power balance seemed irreversibly positioned in favour of Israel. Under the right-wing government of Yitzhak Shamir, more and more Palestinian lands were taken for settlement building, and Israel's military was becoming more intrusive and heavy-handed, making the territories fertile ground for the uprising that followed. At the time, the PLO itself was growing weak in terms of popularity and outreach in the Occupied Territories where stories of the organization's corruption became public knowledge. To the Palestinians under Israeli occupation, the PLO seemed far, corrupt and weak, busy mending its own internal rifts. Israel, indeed, seemed unstoppable and enjoyed international backing especially as the United States' policy at the time was mandated by the globalist debate which considered Israel an asset, militarily, morally and politically (i.e. Israel would curb Soviet penetration and serve as a bastion of order in the region). This translated into an 'Israel First' policy in the US, especially since the Nixon Doctrine encouraged the use of local allies to fend off threats to United States' interests in the region. Therefore, the massive civilian uproar in the Occupied Territories forced Israel to acknowledge the harsh realities of the occupation, tipping the balance in the weaker party's favour. Subsequent events further addressed the power asymmetry, causing both parties to re-evaluate their positions. That is, the end of the cold war meant the end of Soviet financial and military support to radical Arab states, making the goal of supplanting the 'Zionist state' more far-fetched than ever before. It also meant the possibility of denying Israel its special status to the United States in the absence of a Soviet threat in the region. Both parties' stances changed against such a background. The PLO adopted a shift in paradigm, a pragmatic necessity in light of the imminent threat of losing leadership to the Intifada figures or Hamas. It declared its acceptance of a two-state solution and expressed its wish to enter negotiations with Israel on that basis. Israel, coming under fire internally and internationally for its harsh occupation and lured by better economic prospects as a result of peace with the Palestinians, agreed. The result was the Madrid Peace Conference and the peace process that followed, culminating with the Declaration of Principles between the PLO and Israel on 13 September 1993, paving the way for other Arab countries to follow suite and make peace with Israel.

Transformation views economic, religious and patriarchal structures as deep-rooted and objective structures that can be causes for conflict. They yield a 'real clash' of interests as opposed to a perceived one. As such, transformation proponents hold a holistic view of conflict that defines its dynamics as cyclical and dialectic with conflicts manifested and polarized before a structural change (i.e. transformation) could be envisaged. In people-to-people contacts and peace-building, the role of such innate structures is critical and warrants special attention. As explained earlier, the majority of Jordanians wanted formal peace with Israel and probably a warm one after addressing the structural imbalances. Far too many psychological and cognitive obstacles existed to allow envisaging anything but a formal peace especially in a social and political culture (not unique to Jordan) where 'anti-Zionist' and anti-Israeli themes have long been pillars of faith. The structural role of culture, in this context, is highlighted and rightly so.

In a sense, all three main approaches to understanding and resolving conflicts (Realism, conflict resolution and transformation) tend to be either agent- or structure-based. Therefore, the author draws upon insights from all three theories as opposed to choosing one, especially conflict resolution and transformation, which, as this book will prove, are complimentary as opposed to substitutive. As to realism, classic or neo, its insights illuminate interstate interaction in the Jordanian–Israeli context, especially since the elite decision-makers constructed an understanding of the conflict in mostly realist terms.

This analytical basis, however, should not be viewed as embracing contradic-tory concepts given that constructivism forms the philosophical paradigm and methodological/analytical approach adopted in the research at hand. Being a form of post-positivism, constructivism does not mean a slight difference from the positivist position, but rather a rejection of its central tenets. The essence of constructivism is that international relations are social constructions, meaning that facts are theory-laden and contexts matter to political actors since they influence their understanding of conflict and, thus, impact upon their preferences for action and choice within available options. Therefore, it should not be understood as a mere critique of international relations. Nor should it be confused with volun-tarism, implying that we would be able to construct any world simply by wanting it. Rules and norms guide actors in their behaviour; they are inter-subjective, not individual. As such, there is no dichotomy between structure and agency but rather a bridge.

2 The long journey to peace

Jordanian–Israeli relations until the Treaty of Peace of 1994

After tracing the historic background to the conflict and quest for peace at the top-leadership level, the chapter will delve deeper into the psychological dimension of the conflict and its impact on the cognitive and ideological beliefs of the Arab parties concerned, particularly Jordanian. The analysis will permit a better understanding of the turn political events had taken by highlighting the influences on the decision-making process in Jordan and will also explain the roots of the anti-Israeli culture (better known later as the 'anti-normalization movement') identified later in this book as a key obstacle to a warm peace. It is noteworthy that in constructing a historical narrative, reliance was on mainstream English language historiographies.

Historic overview of the conflict up to formal peace[1]

Long before all talk of peace, coexistence and compromise became the norm from the latter half of the twentieth century onwards, Prince (later King) Abdullah accepted the UN partition plan of 1947 expressed in resolution 181, agreeing to live as Arabs and Jews side by side in peace. The realist monarch, however, was held back by the collective Arab resolve to the contrary. Therefore, Jordan took part in the 1948–9 war better known in the Arab World as the 'catastrophe' (*al-Nakbah*). An armistice agreement was later signed between the Hashemite Kingdom of Jordan (the first time that the name had been used) and Israel.[2]

Prince Abdullah was later able to annex the West Bank to Jordan by the Act of Union of April 1950, a union that at the time was met with Arab disapproval. In the subsequent years, Jordan was subjected to hostile propaganda and even faced expulsion from the Arab league. Despite being in the unique position to offer a peace that did not demand the return of the Palestinian refugees, Israel never offered Jordan an adequate peace deal. This is because Israelis were divided on the issue of peace with Jordan and failed to understand that in order to have peace with Israel, Abdullah I needed a generous deal that would justify the peace and vindicate the King's stand, not only before the Arab world but his own people as well. However, Ben-Gurion's lack of commitment to a political settlement was a key factor behind losing a major opportunity for peace with a neighbouring Arab country (Shlaim 2001). Indeed, the Israeli Revisionist historians revealed a wealth of evidence that Israeli decision-makers thought time was on their side; they were strong and the Arabs weak. As such, they could afford to wait and dictate their own uncompromising conditions for peace, which they were not pressed to achieve, anyway, in light of more urgent matters related to state building.

As for Jordan, its first King was assassinated, a heavy price to pay for his policies vis-à-vis the Palestinian question, while the Jordanian government continued undeterred in its unique policy among all Arab states of rehabilitating Palestinian refugees, giving them Jordanian citizenship. The eighteen-year-old Hussein, grandson of assassinated King Abdullah I, acceded to the throne in May 1953 and, like his grandfather, was in favour of peaceful coexistence with the neighbours across the border. A realist and gifted reader of the political charts at home and in the region, he understood from the start that his regime and country stood more to gain from peaceful coexistence than otherwise. Therefore, a de facto peace – albeit a fragile one – prevailed between Jordan and Israel despite the irregular acts perpetrated across the borders against Israelis and the Israelis' retaliatory raids. While these were, at times, symbolic, other times they amounted to massive military operations, seriously undermining the regime stability in Jordan, much to the amazement of King Hussein.[3] One key example is the 1966 massive attack on Samu village, south of Hebron, which resulted in the destruction of forty-one houses and infliction of death upon dozens of Jordanian soldiers.

However, a common source of threat and an act of union did not consolidate King Hussein's claim to represent the Palestinian people in their struggle. The Arab League Summit of 1964 convened in Cairo and issued a collective declaration by Arab states in which they formally stated the destruction of the state of Israel as their ultimate goal. Another historic decision was the establishment of the Palestine Liberation Organization (PLO) to be the representative of the Palestinians in their struggle for independence, a role the Jordanian leadership had hoped to assume.

The Six Day War of 1967 was waged between Israel and Egypt, Jordan and Syria. The dynamics leading up to the war were mostly based upon inter-Arab rivalries (i.e. break-up of the United Arab Republic, Abd al-Karim Qasim, the Yemen civil war morass, etc.) which constituted the background for attacks on Nasser's leadership in the Arab world. Attacked by both the left and right for his inaction on the Israeli front, Nasser was prompted into requesting the redeployment of the UN force in Sinai. In response, the UN Secretary General withdrew UN forces altogether, an act which gained Nasser immediate popular support, reinstating him as an Arab hero. Other factors included Israel's emerging nuclear power (and Egyptian attempts at putting an end to it), Israeli success at diverting the Jordan River water for development of other parts of its state (and continued Syrian efforts to end this project), as well as an emerging Palestinian national movement challenging the Israeli as well as Jordanian societies. Arab fever for military action was increased by certain verbal Israeli declarations that were perceived as displays of pure arrogance. Levi Eshkol, the Israeli prime minister at the time, threatened to hit the Arabs 'where and how we choose' while his chief of staff, Yitzhak Rabin, was reported in Cairo as having said on 12 May that 'We will carry out a lightning attack on Syria, occupy Damascus, overthrow the regime there and come back' (Dallas 1999: 107). Jordan joined the war of 1967 – also known as the War of June – despite serious misgivings about its battle-field prospects. It joined in order to appease pan-Arab and Palestinian opinion that threatened to escalate into fatal domestic challenges to the regime (Gause in Salem 1997: 207, Lunt 1989) and state stability. The war was a military victory for Israel, which was able to annex the West Bank and unite both parts of Jerusalem, and reassert its deterrent power. As the official Israeli narrative holds: three Arab states, including the most powerful, could not defeat a single young state which managed to secure its strategic objectives (namely opening the Straits of Tiran for its navigation and destroying the Egyptian army in Sinai, thereby restoring the image of the deterrent Israeli Defence Force) while claiming moral superiority in the process, portraying its role as purely defensive.

King Hussein played an active role in the war, taken in by the powerful under-currents of Arab nationalism. Pleas against his entering the war failed to find an ear, and Jordanian forces, under Egyptian command, shelled the Israeli side of Jerusalem.

Many historians perceive this as King Hussein's fatal mistake. They argue that had he not intervened in the war, he would have kept the eastern part of Jerusalem and the West Bank, as Israel was not inclined to take any military action against Jordan or annex the densely populated West Bank with Arab inhabitants hostile to Israel. Even though the idea of having the Jordan River as the eastern border of the country was tempting to Israel, the price to achieve it was unattractive as voiced by Rabin, chief of staff at the time (Shlaim 2001). However, it must be noted that the domestic scene in Jordan made it extremely difficult for King Hussein to contemplate inaction, especially against the background of violent demonstrations in Jordan in 1963 (urging Jordan to join the proposed Egypt–Syria–Iraq union) and 1966 (in the wake of the massive Israeli attack on the village of Samu).

In the wake of 1967, Transjordanians and Palestinians felt a deep sense of loss. Transjordanians, most of whom occupied combat units, developed a guilt complex for the tremendous loss, while many Palestinians subscribed to the conspiracy theory claiming that the Jordanian army had not fought hard and that Jordan had conspired to help Israel defeat Nasser and take over more Pales-tinian territories. They overlooked the fact that Jordan lost more than any other Arab country in the battle, with the Kingdom shedding almost half its territory, including East Jerusalem. However, one of the war's most significant outcomes is that Israel's occupation of territories belonging to Jordan, Syria and Egypt created bilateral issues between these states and Israel, causing the three Arab states to reconsider their ultimate purpose of dismantling Israel in favour of negotiating 'land for peace'.

For Israel, the war united both halves of Jerusalem and the borders of the state coincided with those of biblical Israel, giving rise to two competing approaches to resolving the conflict. One saw this as an opportunity to use the newly acquired lands as a basis for establishing peace with neighbouring Arab states, the other was to deem this a divine intervention, further justifying the very existence of the state and awakening dreams of further expansions. Jews who had been reconciled to the idea of a partitioned Jerusalem from 1937 until 1967 – even accepting the UN plan for internalization of the city in 1947 – now perceived Jerusalem as an integral part of *Eretz Israel* (Land of Israel), with many believing it was delivered by divine intervention to serve as the eternal capital of the State of Israel. Consequently, a third form of Zionism (in addition to Labour and Revisionist) emerged, accompanying the birth of a generation that included members whose regard for the Arabs was mostly one of contempt and superiority (Cohen 1990). Israel was confident in its own power and wanted to engage in peace talks with its neighbours immediately following the Six Day War, given its advantageous negotiation position. However, the crushing defeat, deep sense of humiliation, a history of rejected secret and public peace offers and, above all, a very weak negotiation position prevented Arabs from negotiating peace without an Israeli withdrawal from the territories occupied in the war.

In the wake of the war, the UN Security Council issued the famous resolution 242, which emphasized the inadmissibility of the acquisition of territory by force, calling for all-out efforts to achieve a just and lasting peace. It called for the 'withdrawal of Israeli armed forces from territories occupied in the recent conflict' and respect for the right of every state in the area to live in peace within secure and recognized borders. The resolution was considered a masterpiece in deliberate British ambiguity, which, it is believed, won it the support of the United States, the Soviet Union, Jordan and Egypt (but not Syria). It called for withdrawal from 'territories' not '*the* territories' occupied in the recent conflict. This meant that Israel's interpretation of the resolution differed drastically from that of the Arabs. Egypt and Jordan agreed to peace but insisted on Israeli withdrawal first whereas Israel saw withdrawal as conditional to having a contractual peace agreement with these countries that set secure and recognized borders. Even though Israel wanted to resolve the problem of the West Bank, it was not willing to give it up to Jordan. What was on offer was ceding 33 per cent of the West Bank and Eastern Jerusalem, an offer wholly unacceptable to King Hussein. Nor was Israel willing to give it up to the Palestinians themselves, as it wanted to retain sovereignty while offering a form of limited autonomy to the West Bank whose traditional leaders listened to Israeli suggestions and turned them down. This is because no real independence was being offered and therefore any acceptance of the deal would be perceived as a form of betrayal for an unjustifiable outcome.

A sense of Palestinian nationalism was accelerated against the background of crushing defeat. The mounting sense of nationalism coincided with the PLO leadership's realization that liberation would not come from outside (a realization that the Palestinian people came to later in 1987 with the Intifada). Arab states were weaker than Israel and, naturally, guided more by national interests than a pan-Arab strategy. Therefore, it decided to take matters into its own hands, launching Fedayin (Arabic for self-sacrificers) attacks against Israel from confrontation states' borders. One famous confrontation as a result of Fedayin activities took place on 21 March 1968 at al-Karama when Fedayin and Jordanian armed forces engaged the Israeli Defence Force, forcing it to retreat after heavy casualties sustained on both sides. This famous confrontation was later cause for conflict between Jordanians and Fedayins since the latter claimed the sole glory and victory of the battle, despite the fact that the Jordanian armed forces' participation was crucial in forcing the Israeli tanks and heavy artillery to retreat, something Fedayin fighters could not accomplish on their own (Bligh 2000, Abu-Odeh 1999). Fedayin's role brought a structural change in the hierarchy of the PLO as seats were allocated to them in the fourth PNC meeting in Cairo in 1968. A year later, Yasser Arafat was elected as chairman of the PLO's executive committee.

Fatah, a guerrilla group then acting independently of the PLO, had a strategy of dragging Arab states into war with Israel prompted by clashes across the borders of Arab confrontation countries. Jordan and Egypt tried to prevent them from operating across their borders based on the collective Arab states' resolution in the mid-sixties that confrontation with Israel should be postponed until Arab forces could match the Israelis'; consequently, actions by groups that could speed this confrontation should be prevented. However, following the 1967 defeat, the guerrilla organizations were allowed into Jordan, later creating 'a state within a state' for themselves, challenging the rule of King Hussein, resulting in the King ordering his army in 1970 to disarm and break the power of these organizations. This started a civil war at the end of which the remaining fighters left the country for Lebanon and other neighbouring states. At the height of the crisis, Syrian forces entered Jordan in what seemed an attempt to help the Palestinians overthrow the monarchy and take over the country, but in vain.

In 1972, King Hussein unveiled his plan for a United Arab Kingdom, a federation between Palestine (Gaza Strip and the West Bank) and Jordan (the East Bank) with each region having its own government and separate judicial system. Amman would be the capital of the Jordanian region and Jerusalem of the Palestinian region. The PLO and Egypt both refused the plan and Egypt severed its diplomatic relations with Jordan in protest of what seemed proof of secret efforts by King Hussein for a separate peace deal with Israel. The offer threatened the PLO given the continued Israeli refusal to recognize or negotiate with them. Therefore, the Arab League Summit in Morocco's capital, Rabat, nipped King Hussein's idea in the bud by its endorsement of the PLO as 'the sole legitimate representative of the Palestinian people', reconfirming their right to set up an independent national authority led by the PLO on any liberated part of Palestine. This meant that any territory captured in 1967 should not revert to Jordan if liberated but to the Palestinians to establish their state. Had the Israelis agreed to withdraw from the 1967 territories early enough upon King Hussein's repeated requests, the Rabat decision might have been pre-empted.

Overall, Jordan's quest for formal peace with Israel was continuously frustrated. In fact, of all Israeli interactions with Jordan, only one Israeli plan was offered to settle the Jordanian–Israeli conflict: the Allon Plan (named after Deputy Prime Minister Yigal Allon). The plan, while offering Israeli withdrawal from the West Bank in exchange for peace with Jordan, stated that Israel would annex the Jordan Valley on strategic and security grounds, which, unsurprisingly, was met by a Jordanian rejection of the plan. Nothing short of recovering all of the West Bank (including East Jerusalem) would have incited King Hussein to agree. Therefore, when Moshe Dayan later proposed another partition plan between Israel and Jordan, King Hussein rejected it out of hand explaining to Dayan that anything short of a complete Israeli withdrawal would constitute a 'sell-out'. At the same time, King Hussein was receptive to the idea of a territorial swap, provided it was on an equal scale: meter for meter. However, Israeli labour-led governments were not in a position to make generous public and official offers for fear of losing government coalitions, especially since the 1967 war resulted in the radicalization of the National Religious Party (NRP). Furthermore, Israel's primary concern was making peace with Egypt given its leading role in the Arab World. After all, it had a de facto peace with Jordan and was in no hurry to make it de jure.

The October 1973 war, in which Jordan was not a direct participant, brought Jordan closer to the United States, with both supporting UN Security Council Resolution 338 calling on parties involved in the war to cease their hostilities and implement UNSC Resolution 242 of 1967 (which provided for a peace based on Israeli withdrawal from occupied territories). King Hussein's hopes for an eventual return of the West Bank, with the help of the United States, were initially alive but time was not on Jordan's side. Egypt undercut King Hussein, and indeed all Arab states, by signing a peace treaty with Israel. Despite tremendous pressure by the United States on Jordan to join the Camp David Process, it never did. The arrival of Likud to government in 1977 and their leaders' bellicose harangues against Jordan (and especially the adoption by some of its key figures of the idea that 'Jordan is Palestine') constituted a watershed in Jordanian–Israeli relations (Barari 2004) and caused King Hussein to seriously doubt Jordan being able to retrieve the Occupied Territories. As such, Jordan refused to join Camp David and suffered United States' dissatisfaction as a result.[4]

At the Arab League Summit of 1982, the PLO was again confirmed as the sole legitimate representative of the Palestinian people and negotiations with Israel were allowed *only* within a framework of an international conference (a step indicative of Arab states' coming to terms with the existence of the Jewish state in the region). Consequently, King Hussein pursued a double policy of calling for an international conference attended by the permanent members of the UN Security Council while attempting to gain the right to negotiate over the future of the West Bank and Gaza from the PLO itself. Therefore, on 11 February 1985, he concluded an agreement with Arafat on a common approach to a peace process involving Israel. The result was the exercise of Palestinian self-determination through a Palestinian–Jordanian confederation, which meant the formation of a Jordanian–Palestinian delegation to engage in peace talks with Israel at an international conference. The conditions, however, that the PLO had to meet in order to participate in such a conference were still in force ever since Henry Kissinger set them in 1975 as a prerequisite for launching PLO–US talks: to accept Resolution 242, to recognize Israel's right to exist and to renounce violence. The presence of the PLO was a double-edged sword for both Israelis and Jordanians. For King Hussein, the higher the profile of the PLO in negotiations, the less risk regionally or internally, while to the Israelis, the higher the profile of the PLO the harder it would be to rally support for the negotiations internally. In reality, Jordanian–Palestinian cooperation was not a welcome idea within the PLO who objected to such close cooperation with Jordan, renouncing the possible alliance. Therefore, in 1985, in an attempt to force itself upon the negotiations scene, the PLO stepped up its attacks on Israeli targets from within Jordan. Force 17, known as Arafat's bodyguards, killed three Israelis thought to be Mossad agents in Larnaca. Ariel Sharon publicly demanded retaliation against the PLO headquarters in Amman, arguing that King Hussein himself was implicated in the acts, having become Arafat's partner in negotiations. Peres and Rabin, however, did not intend to satisfy Sharon's wishes but had to react nonetheless. The retaliation took the form of a strike by the Israeli Air Force on the PLO headquarters in Tunis. The raid killed fifty-six Palestinians and fifteen Tunisians, wounding some hundred others. Arafat narrowly escaped death. The act was condoned by the US as a legitimate response to terrorism but condemned by the UN Security Council and other member states. Relations between Jordan and the PLO continued to deteriorate and on 19 February 1986 King Hussein, in a public speech that lasted three and a half hours, announced that he was ending his efforts to construct a joint peace strategy with Arafat and the PLO. He characterized Arafat as unworthy and said that the problem lay in his unwillingness to accept Resolutions 242 and 338.

The ending of the joint Jordanian–PLO effort at peace revived within Israel's Labour the 'Jordanian option' to resolving the Palestinian problem. Therefore, Israel did not object to the efforts by King Hussein to further his involvement in the West Bank where he proposed a five-year plan targeting economic improvements. Israel as well as the United States condoned the plan.[5] However, the PLO sent a strong signal of opposition to the plan by killing the pro-Jordanian mayor of Nablus. Consequently, King Hussein closed the offices of the PLO in Jordan, resulting in the expulsion of Abu Jihad (Khalil Al Wazir), PLO's chief of operations and Arafat's deputy. The Jordanian monarch continued to cultivate leadership from the West Bank that would hopefully replace the PLO (which remained opposed to adopting resolutions 242 and 338 and renouncing violence) and be Jordan-friendly. Other measures taken within this context included granting Jordanian citizenship to Palestinians living in the West Bank and paying salaries of Palestinian officials on government payroll before and since 1967. Economic links were strengthened by increased imports from the West Bank, continued extension of development grants and loans to Palestinian firms and provision of government guarantees for private Jordanian loans to West Bank municipalities. Above all, however, was the Israeli-condoned policy of 'open bridges' which allowed visits between family members living in Jordan or the Occupied Territories, conveying a tacit Israeli approval of the Jordanian role in the areas under occupation.

A valuable opportunity for peace was lost with the failure of the London Agreement reached between Peres and Hussein in London in 1987. The agreement consisted of two documents, one detailing the procedures of an international conference at which peace negotiations would commence and another detailing the agreements already reached between Jordan and Israel and which addressed all issues pertaining to the Occupied Territories. Failure to implement the agreement was due not to PLO disapproval but to Peres' inability to obtain approval from his own government, having led King Hussein into thinking that he, Peres, was, in fact, speaking for a united government when working on the terms of the agreement with him. This delivered a blow to King Hussein who, henceforth, saw Peres as someone with whom he could not 'do business'.[6]

In the Occupied Territories, Palestinian hopes had been raised with the London Agreement only to be immediately crushed, increasing feelings of hopelessness as the Palestinians watched more and more of their land and water resources being taken for settlement building and settlers' use under the right-wing led government of Shamir. Israel's military was becoming more intrusive and heavy-handed, making the territories fertile ground for the uprising that followed. The outbreak of the Intifada in 1987 was completely spontaneous. It was the result of mounting frustration by the Palestinians living under occupation, especially since the Arab League summit of 1987 relegated the Palestinian problem to the sidelines, indicating that solution was left to the Palestinians themselves. Transformation of the dynamics of the Arab–Israeli conflict from another angle ensued: the superpowers. The end of the cold war meant the end of Soviet financial and military support to radical Arab states. The goal of supplanting a Jewish Israel was no longer feasible.[7] The PLO itself was also growing weak in terms of popularity and outreach in the Occupied Territories with stories about the organization's corruption becoming common daily topics of discussion. To the Palestinians, their sole legitimate representative was not doing a satisfactory job at ending the Israeli occupation. It was, instead, busy mending rifts between its ranks, especially after Fatah's dissent, an episode that ended with the reunification of the PLO members (Fatah, PFLP, DFLP, CPP) in Algiers in 1987. It also appeared particularly helpless after the air raid on its headquarters by the Israeli Air Force, and very distant after its expulsion from Lebanon. Frustration among people increased given that not even a Jordanian option seemed feasible after the failed London Agreement (Abu-Odeh 1999).

Against such a background, the PLO adopted a shift in paradigm, a pragmatic necessity in light of an imminent threat of losing leadership to Intifada's grass-roots figures or Hamas. It, therefore, agreed to negotiate with Israel on a two-state concept in the hope that by doing so, it would reinstate itself at the head of the struggle in spite of all its failures and shortcomings. The Intifada, which had its roots in poverty, managed in a few months to accomplish what decades of violence and diplomacy had failed to achieve. Perhaps what was remarkable about it was that it meant the end of the myth that the majority of the Palestinians had harboured since 1948 of a saviour coming from outside, a belief strengthened by the Arab League's pledge in the same year to liberate Palestine. The Palestinians, disenchanted with the defeat of 1948, shifted their attention and hopes to Nasser who emerged as a hero after toppling the monarchy in Egypt, nationalizing the Suez Canal Company in 1956 and later by standing up to the tripartite British–French–Israeli attack. The United Nations emerged as a possible saviour through Resolution 242, the Soviet Union as well, being sympathetic with the Arab cause. Nasser's military defeat in 1967, however, was the signal to the PLO that the promise of liberation would not come from outside. An extraordinary summit of the Arab League in Algiers in 1988 reaffirmed the PLO as the sole representative of the Palestinian people in any negotiations and pledged financial and diplomatic support for the uprising. Not only was the PLO's leadership confirmed but the final communiqué of the summit upheld the separation of the two banks by calling for the creation of an independent Palestinian state under the PLO's leadership. Even though Jordan and the PLO had agreed on the eve of the Summit that financial aid allocated for the West Bank would be channelled through both parties, it was decided that only the PLO would serve as channel for financial aid of the Intifada. This was a heavy blow to King Hussein since the Arab states pledging financial support to the Intifada exclusively through the PLO were the same ones that declined to fulfil or renew their Baghdad commitments to Jordan earlier. King Hussein was forced to re-evaluate his position and acknowledge the fact that the Israelis were not about to end the occupation. Therefore, on 31 July 1988, King Hussein suddenly announced that Jordan was severing its legal and administrative ties with the West Bank. Surprisingly enough, leaflet no. 24 of the uprising considered Jordan's disengagement with the West Bank 'the greatest accomplishment of the Intifada'.

The King felt he was fighting a losing battle and after decades of trying to fuse the East and West Banks, he came to the conclusion that it was up to the Palestinians to decide what they wanted to do with the West Bank and to deal directly with the Israelis in the future. In a press conference on 7 August 1998 the King said that Jordan would never again assume the role of negotiations on behalf of the Palestinians. He also said he never liked the Israeli term of 'Jordanian option' as it insinuated a deal with Jordan over the heads of the Palestinians and assured everyone that if the option existed before, it was now formally dead. The stunned Israelis were suspicious of the move by the King and thought it was a tactical move meant to have pro-Jordanian Palestinians show support to the King. However, when the King ordered his supporters in the West Bank not to sponsor petitions for him to relent, they were convinced of the genuineness of the offer. King Hussein was frustrated with the inability to achieve a breakthrough in peace negotiations with Israel and realized that the United States was unlikely to convince Israel to relinquish the Occupied Territories as per UNSC Resolution 242. Above all, Jordan suffered economically (foreign debts in 1988 amounted to US$6 billion), a decrease in foreign aid and rising unemployment levels resulted in the devaluation of the Jordan Dinar by almost 50 per cent at the time.[8] By 1983 (five years before the disengagement), the continued migration from the West Bank to the East Bank was becoming too costly with no visible benefit, especially in light of a deteriorating domestic economy. Amman was also burdened by the allocation of some US$36 million a year in salaries, pensions and stipends for civil servants in the Occupied Territories and as such economic and political frustration were building up, leading to the formal disengagement.

Israel never appreciated King Hussein's need to regain all (not merely parts of) the Occupied Territories to avoid alienating Arab opinion over a peace treaty. Anything less than complete withdrawal would have constituted a sell-out and would have entailed disastrous ramifications given the domestic and overall Arab constraints. Therefore, King Hussein decided to disengage administratively and legally from the West Bank,[9] especially when the Intifada showed the low popularity of a Jordanian role among grass-roots and Intifada leadership. In evidence, the tenth communiqué issued on 11 March 1988, by the United Command of the Uprising called on the people to:

> intensify the mass pressure against the occupation army and the settlers and against collaborators and personnel of the Jordanian regime ... We also call upon the [Palestinian] deputies in the Jordanian Parliament who were appointed by the King to represent our people, to promptly resign their seats and align with their people. Otherwise, there will be no room for them on our land.
>
> (Abu-Odeh 1999: 225)

Not surprisingly, King Hussein found the communiqué to be 'a horrible sign of ingratitude'.

Jordan, it appeared, went back to the former borders of Transjordan as declared by Winston Churchill in the Cairo conference of 1921, a reality seemingly accepted by the formal act of considering the PLO office in Amman (on 7 January 1989) as the embassy of Palestine to Jordan, with a Palestinian ambassador who presented his credentials to the King. Israel now had no one but the PLO to deal with.

The PLO's decision, in Algiers, to accept the relevant UN resolutions going back to 29 November 1947, and to adopt the principle of a two-state solution was indeed historic; one that brought it ahead of Hamas.[10] This meant that the claim to all of Palestine, enshrined in the Palestinian National Charter, was finally laid to rest in favour of establishing a state in the West Bank and Gaza with East Jerusalem as its capital. Israel's decision to hold direct talks with the PLO was truly a diplomatic revolution in Israeli foreign policy, one that paved the way to the Oslo Accords.[11]

The Declaration of Principles (DOP) marked a breakthrough in the century-old conflict between the Arabs and Jews in Palestine. It was initiated, achieved and initialled in Oslo but signed on the south lawn of the White House on 13 September 1993 and marked by the famous handshake between Arafat and Rabin. Until then, Jewish and Palestinian nationalism were exclusive, each denying the other recognition or the right to self-determination. Palestinians have always rejected the idea of a partitioned Jerusalem, when first proposed by the Peel Commission in 1937 then by the UN in 1947. In 1993, however, they had become reconciled to it even though the declaration was completely silent on this vital issue (as well as others including the right of return of the 1948 refugees, borders of a Palestinian entity and the future of Jewish settlements in Gaza and the West Bank). Additionally, the historic significance of the declaration was the subsequent absence of a compelling reason for other parties, especially Jordan, not to seek formal peace with Israel.

Jordan's peace with Israel

An agenda for peace talks between Jordan and Israel had been in place since October 1992, but the King preferred to wait until a breakthrough happened along the Israeli–Palestinian track. On 25 July 1994, President Clinton acted as master of ceremonies and witness to the agreement signed between Jordan and Israel later known as the 'Washington Declaration'. The agreement was not brokered by the United States but was named after the US Capital as a gesture by both parties to President Clinton. In the agreement, both countries agreed to seek a just, lasting and comprehensive peace based on resolutions 242 and 383. The importance of the declaration, drafted at the highest level in Jordan, lay in the fact that it ended the state of belligerence between the two countries, paving the way for serious negotiations, and that it addressed issues of practicality that would, at once, serve as confidence-building measures. These included the establishment of direct telephone links, joint electricity grids, new border crossings giving free access to third-country tourists and cooperation between the police forces in combating crime and drug smuggling. These were in addition to the joint projects promoting tourism, developing the Jordan Rift Valley and constructing a Red Sea Coastal Road. The projects were all announced before the signing of the treaty to raise hopes and pave the way for peace. However, the agreement drove a wedge between Jordan and the PLO as Israel formally undertook to respect the 'special role of the Hashemite Kingdom of Jordan in the Muslim holy shrines in Jerusalem and to give priority to this role when negotiations on final status take place'. This appealed to King Hussein who always made a distinction between religious and political sovereignty over Jerusalem as evidenced by the fact that even when Jordan severed its legal and administrative links with the West Bank in 1988, it maintained them with the Islamic *waqf*. However, this controversial issue constituted a threat to the PLO. Therefore, Arafat immediately embarked on the offensive, calling for immediate negotiations with Israel over Jerusalem, rallying support from the Arab states, seeking Arab League reaffirmation of the PLO's sole rights over the city and adopting such measures as banning the pro-Jordanian newspaper, *al-Nahar*, in Gaza and Jericho (Shlaim 2001).

With the Washington Declaration, Jordan took its chance to establish peace with Israel, being second after Egypt, to sign a full-fledged peace treaty with Israel, but in the unique position of contemplating and indeed speaking of full normalization of relations at all levels. Peace with Israel meant reinstating Jordan in the West's favour, especially after its stance in the Gulf Crisis which brought it regional as well as international isolation not to mention massive economic repercussions estimated at US$1 billion a year (Mango 2003). After his address to the congress following the signing of the declaration, King Hussein obtained a reduction of Jordan's external debt to the United States equal to US$220 million out of a promised US$702 million total.

With the Washington Declaration signed, negotiations of a full-fledged peace treaty between the two countries ensued. While progress was rapid along economic and touristic avenues, it was very slow and difficult on core issues pertaining to Jordan's main strategic objectives, namely borders, water, security and refugees. Nonetheless, these issues were mainly resolved (except for the refugees question) to the satisfaction of both parties.

Overcoming obstacles

Borders

The issue of borders between the two states was particularly difficult to resolve. Both parties agreed earlier in the common agenda signed in September 1993 and subsequent sub-agenda that the borders would be delimited with reference to the Mandate line of 1922 announced by the then British High Commissioner for Palestine.[12] However, Israel expanded the eastern frontier in the late 1960s by almost 360 square kilometres, some of which became Israeli farmland with entire kibbutzim living there or irrigating their farms from water drilled in Jordanian land (Mango 2003). The first key problem was Israel's refusal to acknowledge the 1922 demarcation lines since, in reality, they were never physically implemented and subject to differing interpretations. To break the impasse, a compromise was made. Israel accepted the Mandate line of 1922, restoring Jordanian sovereignty over all its Israeli-occupied territories including al-Baqura in the north, al Ghamr in the South and the Dead Sea Salt Pans.[13] In return, King Hussein agreed that Israeli farmers could continue using the land they had cultivated after it reverted to Jordanian sovereignty in al-Baqura, maintaining ownership rights, while in the South, at al Ghamr, private land use was guaranteed for twenty-five years. Minor land exchanges were agreed upon in other locations along the Wadi Araba and the Dead Sea Salt Pans. In other words, the border agreement returned to Jordan its sovereignty rights without undermining Israeli concerns about their citizens' interests, constituting an ideal solution from a conflict resolution perspective.

Water

On the issue of water, both Israel and Syria had been using more than their allocated share of water from the Yarmouk and Jordan Rivers. The Johnston Plan of 1955 for water use in the region, which assimilated the concerns of both Israel and the Arab League at the time, gave Jordan (East and West Banks) the largest share of the waters of the Jordan basin followed by Israel and then Syria and Lebanon. It was agreed that Israel would limit its use of the Yarmouk River to its original allocated share of 25 million cubic meter (MCM) per year, securing the rest of the flow to Jordan (El-Naser 1998: 13). Concerning the Jordan River, Jordan would be allocated 10 MCM per year of desalinated water in return for Israel's use of a similar amount of water in the south. To compensate for the Kingdom's loss of water from the confluence of the Jordan River with the Yarmouk in winter months due to flooding, it was agreed that this water would be stored in Lake Tiberias, allowing Jordan to benefit from it during summer months. Furthermore, both parties agreed to cooperate in finding sources to supply Jordan with an additional 50 MCM per year of drinkable water within one year from the enforcement of the treaty;[14] they equally agreed to endorse a number of cooperative measures that would alleviate water shortage (e.g. development of existing and new water resources, waste reduction and prevention of contamination in addition to mutual assistance and transfer of information on water-related matters).

Refugees

The issue of refugees, however, remained pending, being dependent on final status negotiations between the PLO and Israel. The treaty, nonetheless, committed Israel to addressing the problem in accordance with the international legitimacy and law, which include relevant UN resolutions on the matter.

The peace treaty was finalized and signed on 26 October 1994 at a border point in the Arava desert, the second treaty concluded between Israel and an Arab state and the first signed in the region. The treaty was as popular in Israel as the preceding Declaration, endorsed by the Knesset by 105 votes to 3 with 6 abstentions. Nonetheless, the King realized that peace took his people by surprise, a reality difficult to accept by many of his Palestinian subjects, which would bring a threat of radicalism and Islamic opposition. What mattered most to him, however, was that peace would be judged by its tangible outcomes and hence the great expectations pinned on the peace dividend. Interestingly enough, the agreement did not include a pledged amount in aid on a yearly basis, as was the case with the Israeli–Egyptian peace brokered by the United States.

President Clinton spoke to the Jordanian Parliament endorsing the peace process and pledging his country's support in writing off US$702 million, the total of Jordan's debt to the United States. To King Hussein, however, the peace achieved crucial strategic objectives, more pressing than the peace dividend, which he expected to increase over the years. Abdul Salam Majali, former Jordanian prime minister who signed the treaty on behalf of Jordan, summarized by saying that the treaty formalized Jordan's right to exist and 'buried the *watan al-badeel*' (substitute homeland) option (Abu-Odeh 1999), while safeguarding the Palestinian refugees' rights by obtaining official Israeli acknowledgement of the need to resolve the matter in accordance with international laws,[15] making the peace treaty King Hussein's 'crowning achievement' (Robins 2004: 187).

The historic survey of the conflict and subsequent peace between both states discussed so far indicate that formal bilateral peace remained elusive until 1994. From a Jordanian point of view, this was the result of three factors: Israeli intransigence, Arab and Palestinian constraints. The Arab constraint was largely removed after Egypt signed a treaty of peace with Israel (setting a precedent) and completely disappeared when Arab states (especially Syria and Egypt) joined the US-led coalition against Iraq following its occupation of Kuwait. The Palestinian constraint, however, was largely gone after the PLO signed the Declaration of Principles in September 1993. Before that, making peace with Israel would have been akin to a suicide attempt by the regime (especially without retrieving the whole of the occupied territories, including East Jerusalem). To the mainstream thinking of both East Bank Jordanians and citizens of Palestinian origin, Israel was planted in the region by the colonial powers to subjugate and humiliate the Arabs, prevent their unity and rob them of their lands' natural resources and basic rights. These beliefs were accentuated and lent credibility by the Israeli policies of massive retaliation following border incursions, open-fire practice, establishing facts on the ground and defeating the Arab armies. Moreover, Jordan is home to some 1.7 million refugees, making any move on the peace front without coordination with the Palestinian leadership or resolution of the refugee question impossible. Indeed, Jordan never had a peace offer tempting enough to make an agreement with Israel worthwhile or a deal that would be deemed courageous and honouring as opposed to a formal recognition of defeat.

The conflict in psychological terms

A common challenge in peacebuilding is relationship building, a painful process given the need to learn to view the other as something other than a deadly enemy. This requires a restructuring of dominant perceptions (or rather misperceptions) and rooted beliefs. Therefore, the dominant ideological and cognitive beliefs held by the parties in general and Jordanians in particular must be explained as they contributed to the mainstream images of self, the 'other' and overall political culture, all being formidable challenges peacebuilding had to contend with later on.

Dominant Israeli and Arab frames

Jewish history in the diaspora greatly influenced Israel founding fathers' foreign policy orientation. Zionism[16] emerged as the answer to the problem of the Jewish people who were dispersed around the world, constituting a minority wherever they were. Failure of the Jews to become assimilated in the Western society and mounting anti-Semitism, in tandem with an upsurge in nationalism, gave rise to Modern Zionism in the late nineteenth-century Europe. Returning to *Zion* (i.e. one of the biblical names for Jerusalem) and attaining majority status there was the Zionists' ideal solution and the best way of forming a nation-state similar to the European model, which they saw growing around them in the West, but excluding them (Shlaim 2001). Zionism succeeded in rallying international support for its cause culminating in UN Resolution 181 of 1947 which gave international legitimacy to the partitioning of Palestine for the purpose of creating an independent Jewish state. The trauma of the Holocaust made it all the more crucial for Jews to have a state of their own. In order to overcome local resistance by Palestinians already living in mandatory Palestine, Ze'ev Jabotinsky's ideas on the matter were adopted. The ardent Jewish nationalist (1880–1940) believed in the cultural superiority of the Western civilization, to which the Jews belonged, and legitimacy of the Zionist ambition. He argued that a voluntary agreement with the Arabs would not be possible, concluding that if Zionism was to exist, Zionists would have to settle the Jews under the protection of force behind an iron wall which the Palestinians would be powerless to break. To him and everyone else who subscribed to his views, the moral dimensions of such an approach paled in comparison to the subsequent horrors of the Holocaust.

In the process, the military victories of Israel helped make the 'iron wall' philosophy mainstream among Israeli elite-leadership who for once saw the advantage of military action over diplomacy and negotiation. In short,

> To brook nothing, tolerate no attack, cut through Gordian knots, and shape history by creating facts seemed so simple, so compelling, so satisfying that it became Israel's policy in its conflict with the Arab World.
>
> (Nahum Goldman as cited in Shlaim 2001: 40)

Over-confidence occasionally bordered on arrogance. For example, Syrian President Husni Zaim's famous offer in 1949 to skip armistice talks altogether and proceed directly with negotiating a peace treaty with an exchange of ambassadors, open borders and normal economic relations was rejected out of hand by Ben-Gurion who refused to meet with Zaim to discuss the matter. Ben-Gurion refused even though Zaim was proposing to settle 300,000 Palestinian refugees in northern Syria, asking, in return, for half the Sea of Galilee.

Underlying the arrogant attitude was a deep mistrust tainting Israel's founding fathers' perceptions, making them suspicious of the Arabs around them, about whom, interestingly enough, they knew little and yet enough to distrust them. In more recent history this distrust prompted Israel, for example, not to acknowledge Arafat's 1989 breakthrough declarations. Having been refused an entry visa by the US to address the UN Council, Arafat addressed instead the UN European headquarters in Geneva presenting a three-point peace initiative calling for an international UN sponsored peace conference, a comprehensive settlement based on the relevant UN resolution as well as a UN peacekeeping force to supervise Israeli withdrawals from the Occupied Territories. He also reiterated the condemnation of terrorism that he made earlier at the nineteenth Palestinian National Council (PNC) in Algiers.[17] His press conference declarations of recognizing Israel, accepting UNSC Resolution 242 and renunciation of terrorism were met by Yitzhak Shamir's dismissal of the speech and its declarations as a 'deceitful act of monumental proportions' made with the intention of creating an 'illusion of growing moderation' (Mango 2003: 49).

Indeed, one cannot study Israeli foreign policy without noting the impact of Jewish history, especially the Holocaust before which other tragic Jewish experiences in the diaspora dwindle. According to numerous surveys and studies, most Israelis see the world as a hazardous place where people are basically evil and dangerous. The intentions of Arabs are viewed in a very pessimistic light. Fear of a repetition of the genocide experience is alive, a real possibility. As such, 'Israeli leaders display an exceptionally low threshold of threat reception. The worst is always expected, and a tendency to hysteria on security issues is sometimes concealed with difficulty' (Cohen 1990: 39). Israeli leaders feel a huge responsibility of saving what they consider the 'surviving remnant' of their people with no room for error. At historic meetings between Israelis and Arabs the theme of extermination is present, the fear of a recurrence apparently still haunting the collective memory of Jews, revived by threats of annihilation by chemical warfare from Iraq during the Gulf War in 1990 and Islamist extremist groups even *after* peace. The situation being such, the idea that Arabs wanted nothing but the destruction of Israel, seemed to many (especially Prime Minister Shamir) the very purpose of the Intifada and reconfirmed with Palestinian leadership's public support of the right of return of the refugees, which would spell the demise of the Jewish state. This imminent sense of threat made anything permissible for the sake of saving Jews in peril, hence overlooking such constraints as international law or state sovereignty as exemplified by the commando raids on Entebbe, the bombing of PLO headquarters in Tunis and Beirut and the demolition of Iraq's Osirak nuclear reactor.

Israeli suspicion and over-reliance on military prowess translated into a series of violent retaliations and reprisals across the borders of neighbouring states. Many Palestinian refugees would infiltrate the borders to look for relatives, recover material possessions or, sometimes, exact revenge. Israel's policy of retaliation was disproportionately aggressive and harsh, aiming at making an example of the villages from where infiltrators came. The policy of deterrence demanded that terror be struck in the heart of the Arab public to make the mere idea of fighting Israel inconceivable in light of the massive damage and loss it would entail. Consequently, Israel adopted a 'free-fire' policy (meaning shooting first and then asking questions) resulting in the killing of almost 5,000 infiltrators between 1949 and 1956, most of whom were unarmed (Shlaim 2001: 82). The West Bank villages of Falama and Sharafat in 1951 were subject to full-scale attacks by the Israeli Defence Force

(IDF) as a form of collective punishment for suspicion of helping infiltrators. The attack by organized army battalions targeted civilian populations, a policy which inflamed hatred among Arab publics and met with international criticism.

Rosati (1995) argued that different images of the enemy existed of which a 'degenerate' stereotype supported an expansionist attitude in foreign policies, which, from an Arab perspective, could explain Israel's founding fathers' pursuit of expansionist policies. Israel never failed to inflict the worst feelings of shame and helplessness upon the Arab populace through its repeated incursions, reprisals and attacks. Consequently, Arabs' overall sense of victimization and inability to shape their own destiny (what is known as the 'post-Ottoman Syndrome') were deepened by the repeated defeats and Israeli intransigence. The Arab populace, in general, believed that the Israelis held them in contempt. At the same time, the Israeli public felt, despite the state's superior military apparatus, vulnerable and bereft in a sea of 'hostile Arabs', reliving the religious Jewish prediction that time after time, there will emerge those who try to perish them. Clearly, security remained elusive to both parties in the bloody conflict.

The plight of the Palestinians and massive numbers of refugees (the 1948 war alone produced over 500,000 refugees of a population estimated at 900,000 at the time) damaged Arab pride. It fed pan-Arabism whose appeal, after all, was never military, rather ideological, serving as a source for legitimacy, bridging the gap between the externally imposed material structures (e.g. fragmented Arab states) and supra-national Arab/Muslim identity, ending the dissonance (Hinnebusch 2003: 63). Thus, media warfare was launched by Arab states competing in their anti-Israeli sentiment to further prove their Arab credentials and loyalty to the overall sacred cause, thereby appeasing domestic calls for action. Radio Cairo, in particular, excelled at the attempt with its flamboyant rhetoric and public vows that 'the Arab nation is determined to wipe Israel off the face of the earth and restore to Palestine the Arab honour'. Needless to say, such rhetoric enforced the 'Holocaust Syndrome' to which very few Israelis were immune (Cohen 1990). Though the Arab public who were eager for a military victory over Israel lived through a crushing defeat in 1967 of tremendous magnitude, this was not reason enough for them to accept Nasser's resignation from office. People in the Occupied Territories actually begged him not to resign. To them, Nasser was not defeated by Israel alone but by the Western superpowers that sided with Israel. His resignation would therefore symbolize the defeat of the Arab masses. Thus, he had to stay in office, for their collective sake (Abu-Odeh 1999). Not surprisingly, the defeat of 1967 was called *al-nakseh* (Arabic for setback) suggesting a victorious attempt later. It was not defeat but a mere setback. The post-Ottoman syndrome was aggravated by the repeated Arab defeats at the hands of Israel and the more recent US intervention in the Gulf War and war on Iraq. People generally saw the latter as a demonstration of the superpower's ability to 'smash a place up' before going home to celebrate victory, not to mention the deterioration along the peace track and failed attempts at securing Arab rights stipulated in official agreements with Israel. This fostered an atmosphere in which Islamism could promote itself as the ultimate substitute for 'failed' ideologies (especially pan-Arabism), growing stronger as a form of self-preservation and defence, a means for recreating a glorious history under unity where fragmentation along colonially imposed borders and external imposition would no longer be acceptable.

Dominant Jordanian frames: images of self and the other

The Popular Level

Ideological beliefs of the Palestinians were a mixture of nationalism, pan-Arabism and an amalgam of Third World style ideas of social, economic and politico-military revolution. The pan-Arab nationalism of Nasser appealed to them to the extent that, initially, he was more in charge of the Palestinian question than its own leadership. After all, it was Nasser's initiative to create the PLO in 1964, and consequently, for many years, no distinct Palestinian identity was apparent. However, with the crushing defeat of 1967, the Palestinian militia groups decided to take matters into their own hands, believing that only they could liberate their land. A key accomplishment of theirs was reviving a sense of a distinct Palestinian identity to unite the refugees wherever they were in the diaspora. Also part of the Palestinian leadership's ideological belief system was the notion of fighting oppression and colonialism.

On the leadership side, Yasser Arafat viewed his people's struggle as being part of every struggle against imperialism, injustice and oppression in the world; part of a world revolution targeting social justice and liberation for all humanity (Aggestam 1999: 64). Enemy images (the product of cognitive and ideological beliefs) were, as Attribution theory would argue, intimately linked with self-images in an interaction of mutual contingency. Since Zionism was perceived as a racist, expansionist and colonial power, it became imperative to negate Israel as a legal entity. It was understood as a political movement working against the liberation of other people. Therefore, 'Israel' was never mentioned by name but referred to repeatedly as the 'Zionist entity' by the top figures of the Palestinian leadership. The *nakbeh* (Arabic for catastrophe, used to refer to the war of 1948–9) and massacres of Palestinian civilians at Dir Yasin, Sabra, Shatila, and Tal al-Za'tar formed the core of the Palestinians' collective agony. According to Khalidi:

> If the Arab population of Palestine had not been sure of their identity before 1948, the experience of defeat, dispossession and exile guaranteed that they knew what their identity was very soon afterwards: they were Palestinians.
>
> (Aggestam 1999: 63)

The refugees, in particular, felt that the need for an acknowledgement by Israel of the role it played in creating their problem was fundamental and common. They remain faithful to 'helping the dream come true' (a phrase commonly used when discussing the right of return). According to the International Crisis Group (Middle East report no. 22), 'virtually every Palestinian interviewed insisted on recognition as a precondition for a settlement, stating, in the words of Bassam Salhi, leader of the Palestinian People's Party (PPP) that 'without it the problem will never disappear; the rest is details" (ibid: 11). However, a comprehensive Israeli acknowledgement of responsibility is highly unlikely. Zionism, after all, had as a unifying motivating theme 'a land without people for a people without land'. As such, official Israeli history undermines the presence of a Palestinian population/people in mandatory Palestine prior to the establishment of the state of Israel. Arab inhabitants living in Palestine at the time were ignored even though they constituted almost 90 per cent of the population. Former Israeli Prime Minister Levi Eshkol wondered: 'What are Palestinians? When I came here [to Palestine] there were 250,000 non-Jews, mainly Arabs and Bedouins. It was desert, more than underdeveloped. Nothing' (Aggestam 1999: 60). Golda Meir publicly denied the presence of a Palestinian people or identity arguing that 'there is no Palestinian people wandering in the world without knowing where to go' (Chomsky 2003: 132). Israelis further support their argument by stating that no formal Palestinian state existed prior to 1948 in the first place. Israeli documentary evidence apparently exists indicating that those Palestinians left at the invitation of the Mufti who envisaged an Arab aggression that would result in the throwing of all Jews into the sea, destroying the nascent Jewish state (Aggestam 1999: 60–1). The problem of Palestinian refugees, also according to the Israeli official version of events, rests entirely with the Arab states that waged the war and asked Arab inhabitants to leave Palestine to return once the war was over and Jews destroyed or thrown into the sea. Therefore, the idea of repatriation of the refugees was considered absurd especially when Arab inhabitants of Palestine could be easily accommodated within the Arab states, given their territorial superiority. Even a 'dove' like Shulamit Aloni of the Meretz Party describes the right of return as 'less than a dream' (Joffé 2002: 175).

The exodus of hundreds of thousands of Palestinians as refugees into neighbouring Arab states became a threat to some of these states, particularly Jordan and Lebanon. At first, integration between both communities in Jordan was smooth given the presence of unifying social and political values. The magnitude of the Palestinian plight heightened the Jordanian public's sense of duty and obligation towards their fellow Arab brethren in distress. Therefore, any sentiments of disenfranchisement by their government in favour of the West Bank and its development after the act of union in 1950 remained dormant and unvoiced.[18] The creation of the PLO, however, caused a rift in the identity and loyalty of the Palestinians who had already formed sentimental attachments to Jordan, arousing Jordanian fears given the large number of Palestinians among them and in the West Bank. This was compounded by the fact that many Palestinians were not averse to turning Jordan into a Palestinian state. In 1970–1, Palestinian guerrilla groups had their chance and failed, helping a distinct Jordanian/ East Bank political identity crystallize and mature. Jordanian mindset, initially characterized by fear of Israeli expansion, a deep sense of helplessness at losing the West Bank in 1967 and overall Arab inability to restore lost territory and pride, later became fearful of a mounting threat to their political identity as well as state and regime survival. Understandably, they understood the answer to their problem to be primarily in settling the Palestinian–Israeli conflict and maintaining a strong military and security power-base to curb any domestic or external threat. Jordanian Prime Minister Abdul Salam Majali pointedly remarked in this context after the conclusion of the peace treaty with Israel, 'We have buried al-watan al-badil'. Indeed, the treaty of peace sought a commitment to recognizing and respecting Jordan's sovereignty, territorial integrity and political independence, ensuring future absence of threat or use of force against it and avoiding as much as possible involuntary mass movements of people in a way that would prejudice the kingdom's security.[19]

The Elite Leadership

Given the interest this study has in the role of leadership in dealing with the obstacles to a warm peace between Jordan and Israel, it is important to analyse the cognitive and ideological beliefs of Jordan's King Hussein and his successor King Abdullah II, both of whom ruled during the period of concern to this work. This is in light of the monarch's constitutional role in shaping the country's domestic and, more importantly, foreign policy.

King Hussein's ideological beliefs were rooted in an Islamic, Hashemite tradition and a sense of Arabism. Evoking these themes, King Hussein would continuously allude to the Arab Revolt in addition to three pride-inspiring factors: Jordan was the custodian of the Holy Shrines in East Jerusalem (which the Jordanian army bravely defended alongside Palestinian combatants in 1948); Jordan represented a successful attempt at the yearned-for Arab unity; and last, Jordan held the longest lines of confrontation with Israel. Naturally, these themes were present in most of King Hussein's speeches. In essence, the Hashemite heritage served as a supra-national theme and source for unity between Arabs and Muslims. Accordingly, the King would repeatedly refer to his own lineage and the prophet's son-in-law and 'guided' caliph, Ali Bin Abi Taleb (ruled 656–61) as the personal, ideological and historical pillars of the Hashemite dynasty. Indeed, King Hussein's ideological beliefs were not very different from that of his grandfather. However, King Hussein's cognitive beliefs were greatly influenced by the lessons learned from his grandfather's life and, more importantly, death. He learned early on that he could not live outside the political culture otherwise the price could be too high. He therefore declined to join the Camp David talks, knowing that he stood more to lose than win by a premature peace treaty that would alienate him domestically and regionally and prove useless, given his doubts about regaining all of the Occupied Territories. While his ideological beliefs and ambitions led him to compete with the PLO over representation of the Palestinian people, supported by the fact that he had the largest number of Palestinian refugees in his country, it was his cognitive beliefs, however, that prompted him to relinquish the West

Bank. This was the result of a mounting PLO role, accompanied by failure to establish strong functional allies to help make peace with Israel, not to mention his waning popularity among the leadership of the Intifada and dire economic burdens shouldered by Jordan's troubled economy. The severing of all administrative and legal links between Jordan and the West Bank in 1988 was a pragmatic decision made against the background of calculations of loss and gain and future prospects. However, it did not mean a dramatic change in his ideological beliefs as was testified by the fact that he still kept the *Waqf* staff in Jerusalem on Jordanian payroll and welcomed the special role awarded by Israel in the peace treaty.

King Abdullah II who acceded to the throne in February 1999 shared similar cognitive and ideological beliefs. King Abdullah's reading of the political charts encouraged him not to rouse the ire of the West, especially the United States, as not only is Western favour necessary for the country's political stability, but also for the country's economic well-being. He learned the lessons from his father's decision in 1990–1 to side with Iraq (and the consequences both King and country suffered therefore) and subsequent coexistence with the anti-normalization movement and was careful not to make mistakes. Therefore, King Abdullah II showed his lack of tolerance towards proponents of radical and anti-peace ideologies lest their continued fervent activism weaken Jordan's international standing and chances at securing increased financial aid, which the country badly needed. A few months after assuming his powers, he expelled three Hamas leaders from Amman, closing Hamas offices. This signalled a further severing of ties between Jordan and the West Bank (since Hamas is a Palestinian organization) and indicated a staunch position in combating violence and its perpetrators whose actions, he believed, had negative ramifications on the entire region. The King remained undeterred in his policies, freezing the accounts of six Hamas members in September 2001 (albeit unfreezing them soon after in response to massive public outcry) and later siding with the United States in its anticipated 'war on terror'. Overall, the policies pursued by King Abdullah II indicated a tremendous similarity between his cognitive and ideological beliefs and those of his father. The more zealous approach in pursuing these policies, however, may be attributed to his character and impatience for positive achievements in a troubled region.[20]

The Islamic Opposition

The oppositions' leaders echoed the ideological beliefs held by their parties. Since it was mostly the Islamic opposition that spearheaded the anti-normalization movement in Jordan (as will be later explained), the ideological beliefs of the Muslim Brotherhood's local party (i.e. the Islamic Action Front) need examining.

The Islamic Action Front's ideology holds that Jordan has a special role to play in the liberation of Palestine, arguing that Jordan is indeed the 'land of mobilisation and constancy' (*ardh al-hashd wa al-ribat*). This religious perspective is derived from the prophet's saying (i.e. *hadith*) that Muslims would fight and defeat the Jews one day before the end of the world, and that the place of Muslims would be on the east side of the Jordan River while the Jews would be on the west side (i.e. the so-called East and West Banks of the Jordan River). Most reported sayings of the Prophet speak of the battle but do not specify a location. Only the *hadith* conveyed by Nur al-Din Ali al-Haythami (d. AD 807) in his *Majma' al-zawa'id wa manba' al-faw'id* does. Muslim Brotherhood's literature upholds this prophecy, repeated by its leaders and followers who accept peace with Israel in terms of a temporary truce only and until Muslims are strong enough to fight and defeat them, but not as a permanent state of affairs.[21] They acknowledge Arab weakness and condone that the battle would be launched once strength and power were on their side. Even though they acknowledge Judaism as a divine religion and admit that Jews existed in Palestine before the establishment of the Israeli state, they do not look favourably at Jews as they are considered as 'God's adversaries' and 'defilers of the prophets'. With time, the distinction between Judaism and Zionism became blurred with the Brotherhood portraying the conflict as one between two opposing civilizations upholding opposing religions (al-Khazendar 1997: 140). After all, Zionism linked itself to Judaism, building on the premise that Palestine is the land of Israel to be redeemed from non-Jews for all Jews, a belief enshrined in the Israeli Law of Return of 1950 enabling any Jew in the world to return to Israel and obtain citizenship. Therefore, Islamists consider the liberation of the whole of Palestine and dismantling of the Jewish theocratic state, the very 'symbol of Zionism', a divine duty of all Muslims and not only of a particular government. After all, it has Jerusalem, the first *Qiblah* (Muslims' first prayer orientation before Mecca) and the third most sacred shrine in Islam, which makes it sacrilegious to contemplate giving away an inch thereof. It follows that bargaining over the land is unacceptable with concessions made viewed as mere injustices to future Muslim generations. The link between Islam and Palestine also supported a link between Islam and all things Arab to the extent that the Arab culture is defined in Islamic terms (i.e. 'The Arab and Muslim Culture' or 'The Arab and Muslim Nation'). Consequently, most Arab Christians consider themselves belonging to both (Said 1995). The situation being such, the slogan used by the Islamist movement 'Islam is the solution' enjoyed more credibility than the Leftist movement, whose credibility and power of the 1950s and 1960s, once lost, was never fully regained.

Conclusion

As intended, the chapter presented a historic overview of the Jordanian–Israeli relations up to the peace treaty in 1994, within an Arab context in general and a Jordanian–Palestinian one in particular. It examined the conflict from a sociopsychological perspective in order to explain the additional constraints on the decision-making process hindering an earlier Jordanian–Israeli peace. More importantly, the historic analysis exposed the backdrop against which a warm peace was to be pursued, as the coming chapters will discuss in detail.

3 Achieving and building peace (1994–2003)

Jordanian hopes after peace were high as the treaty did not only restore Jordanian rights but also constituted the blueprint for bilateral social, economic and cultural cooperation, that is full normalization of relations. Consolidating these hopes was the growing affinity between King Hussein and Rabin. Formal diplomatic relations between the two countries were established on 11 December 1994 with the opening of embassies in Amman and Tel Aviv. By 30 January 1995, Israel had evacuated 344 square kilometres of Jordanian territories, withdrawing from Aqaba-Eilat to al-Ghamar region in Wadi Araba. The second stage of withdrawals was from al-Baqura, giving Jordan full sovereignty over its territories as early as 10 February 1995 (Mango 2003). Demarcation of borders was completed with the installation of concrete pillars at specific points, a task completed by July of the same year; the maritime border agreement set a median line as an international line between the two states, thereby resolving all issues related to borders between both states.

A security agreement was signed on 9 February 1995. It was special in being the first security agreement between Israel and an Arab state that did not involve a third party (the UN or a multinational force) – clearly the result of a long track of quiet and mature diplomacy.

Cooperation in the field of tourism (Jordan's second source of revenue after the phosphate and potash mining industries) offered Jordan a valuable potential for increasing its income. According to official Jordanian statistics, over 10,000 Israeli tourists visited Jordan in 1994, over 100,000 in 1995 while an average of 120,000 Israelis visited the country yearly in 1996, 1997 and 1998, increasing Jordan's revenue from JOD406.4 million in 1994 to JOD575 million in 1998.

On the economic front, the Jordanian Parliament approved the cancellation of laws prohibiting normal economic relations with Israel by a vote of 51 to 29. The laws included law 66 of 1953 banning trade with Israel, the Unified Boycott Law of 1958 adopted in line with the Arab economic boycott of Israel, and the 1973 law prohibiting sale of land or property to Israelis. One of the highlights of the first year of peace was Jordan's hosting of the second Middle East and North Africa Summit (MENA) in Amman at the end of October 1995, with American and Russian co-sponsorship and support of the European Union, Canada and

Japan. Hundreds of government and business leaders attended the summit whose primary goal was to develop effectively the region's potential through, inter alia, trade liberalization, privatization and capital markets. On the heels of the 1994 Israeli–Jordanian peace treaty, meetings between Israeli, Palestinian and Jordanian businessmen were highly encouraged with the logic being that Arab–Israeli links would strengthen the private sector, a natural supporter for peace and a bulwark against radicalism (Robins 2004: 186). The 1995 Amman Economic Summit witnessed the creation of the Regional Business Council (RBC), managed by Americans to act as a chamber of commerce, facilitating meetings, multilateral exchanges and joint business ventures among leading Jordanian, Israeli and Palestinian business groups. As an incentive, the United States offered the Quali-fied Industrial Zones (QIZ) programme. To Jordan, the summit was a success despite a public argument between the Jordanians and the Egyptians over rapid normalization with Israel. The Egyptian Foreign Minister's speech at the opening session warned against rapid normalization (*harwala*[1]) before a Palestinian state was a reality on the ground, and before Israeli withdrawal from Syrian and Leba-nese territories as well as the removal of the threat of weapons of mass destruction from the region. Jordan considered Amr Musa's speech an attempt to undermine the summit's success. King Hussein therefore seized the chance to remind the Egyptians that while they warned against separate negotiations with Israel, they signed a separate peace treaty with them, breaking from Arab ranks some two decades ago (ironically, the MENA Summit held a year later was actually in Cairo). Commercial ventures estimated at US$100 million were entered into as a direct result of the Summit in addition to the conception of such institutions as the Bank for Economic Cooperation and Reconstruction in the Middle East and North Africa, the Regional Tourism Board and the Regional Business Council in addition to the economic summit secretariat. The summit hailed a new era for Jordan by restoring its good relations with the Gulf States with Saudi Arabia approving the appointment of a Jordanian ambassador to Riyadh towards the end of 1994.

In the first year of peace, a set-back occurred when Rabin approved a plan to confiscate 52 hectares of Palestinian-owned land in East Jerusalem for the expansion of Jewish housing, a decision that sparked heavy criticism from Amman where Parliamentarians started calling for abrogating the treaty of peace and summoning Jordan's ambassador from Tel Aviv. However, King Hussein opted to use his friendship with Rabin to dissuade the latter from his plans. Thus, King Hussein sent Rabin a letter in which he explained the gravity of the situation, urging him to reconsider his decision, which Rabin did and swiftly abandoned his plan (Andoni 1995).

However, the first serious setback to the peacebuilding process occurred with the assassination of Prime Minister Rabin, Israel's war hero, peacemaker and Nobel Laureate. The polarization within Israel culminated in the assassination of Rabin at a rally for peace in Tel-Aviv at the hands of Yigal Amir, a law student at Bar-Ilan University. The twenty-five-year-old assassin belonged to a generation of the Six-Day war who saw in Israel's victory a divine intervention and permanent deed to the land, an ideology commonly shared among religious-nationalists who believed themselves to be the rightful owners of the promised land of Israel. In their view, Arabs are an eternal enemy, when they talk of peace, they should never be trusted since their goal is to retrieve lands occupied in 1967 and wage their war of Jewish annihilation immediately afterwards (Shlaim 2001: 549). The 1967 annexation had led to the emergence of 'religious Zionism' whose adherents believed that the conquest of the West Bank, which as Judea and Samaria formed part of the biblical Jewish kingdom, proved they were living the messianic era, meaning that salvation was at hand. To many orthodox rabbis, the land was delivered through an act of divine intervention, which is why immediately afterwards, many of them began to sanctify the land of their ancestors, making it the object of religious passion. Sanctity of the land became a central tenet of religious Zionism; therefore, anyone giving pieces of it away was a traitor and enemy of the entire Jewish people. Consequently, settlement bore a religious connotation to the religious right wing supported by Likud who long cultivated the image of a vulnerable Israel destined to live by the sword. While the same belief was cultivated earlier by Labour, the latter's foreign policy since 1967 was pragmatic; Likud's, however, remained ideological. Labour's policies were primarily dictated by security considerations but Likud's were by ideology even when security considerations deemed it possible to relinquish territories occupied in the 1967 war. To Likud, integrity of the homeland '*Shlemut Hamoledet*' is a summary of the party's foreign policy. Not only did Rabin discard this policy, but he also challenged the thinking behind it. However, he underestimated the level of polarization within his society. He had outlawed fanatic religious parties like Kach and Kahane Chai after the Hebron massacre, but apparently did not anticipate violence from other extreme edges of the right against Jews. Ironically, in 1967 Rabin had been a hero to the religious right for actively taking part in liberating parts of the historic homeland; in 1993, however, he became a traitor. To King Hussein, the assassination of Rabin was a serious setback to the peacebuilding process, which he hoped would grow stronger with time.

With Peres succeeding Rabin as both prime minister and minister of defence, the relationship between Jordan and Israel kept cooling down. Despite both leaders' earlier contacts, King Hussein had little trust in Peres given that the latter let him down on two particular occasions. The first was when Peres, acting as foreign minister, reached the London Agreement with the King while not speaking on behalf of a united government as King Hussein had thought; the second was leaking to the press news of a secret meeting in Amman with the King in November 1993, telling them to 'remember November 3rd'. The declaration came as Jordan was preparing for its Parliamentary elections, placing the King in an awkward situation and threatening to radicalize the elections' outcome. Above all, perhaps, is the fact that Peres was the architect of the Oslo Accord reached without Jordan's knowledge or regard to its vital interests. Moreover, King Hussein realized that to Peres, peace with Syria and economic integration between Israeli and Palestinians markets were more of a priority than building peace with Jordan. Supporting this view was the decline in water-sharing and economic cooperation between the two states. Jordan's exports to the Occupied Territories were restricted for security reasons, while Jordan believed the true reasons to be self-serving for Israel to whom the Occupied Territories were a captive market. Most alarming to Jordan, though, was Peres' government attempt to reach an agreement with *Waqf*'s Palestinian administration in Jerusalem regarding a tunnel underneath the Haram al-Sharif (known as Solomon's stables) bypassing the Jordanian *Waqf* administration, thereby undermining Jordan's special role in the holy city as recognized in the Treaty of Peace. With the Grapes of Wrath operation in southern Lebanon, however, the deterioration in relations took a dive.

Peres took certain decisions whose repercussions cost him the elections in 1996. He authorized the assassination of Yahya Ayyash, Hamas's so-called engineer who masterminded several suicide attacks, considered by the Israeli media at the time as public enemy number one. It would seem that Peres was aware of his (and his government's) precarious hold on power as was shown by the narrow margin of votes he obtained at Knesset following Rabin's assassination. He wanted to be remembered for a spectacular success, hence the idea of killing Ayyash by means of a booby-trapped cellular phone. Immediately, Hamas declared Ayyash a martyr and promised revenge, blowing up a bus in Jerusalem killing all passengers. Three other attacks followed in Ashkelon, Jerusalem and Tel Aviv damaging Peres's credibility and that of his government. For the first time since Rabin's death, public polls put Likud's Netanyahu ahead of Peres. As a result of these retaliation attacks, Peres suspended talks with Syria on the basis of harbouring terrorists (i.e. the Popular Front for the Liberation of Palestine and others).

A conference in Sharm El Sheikh was convened to discuss terrorism at which King Hussein spoke of the need for a correct understanding of Islam as a religion of tolerance and peace calling for development and better future for all, expressing feelings of sorrow towards those misguided into believing that violence against innocent civilians was a form of Jihad. However, an Israeli–Turkish military cooperation agreement was signed in 1996, presenting a major threat to Syria and Iran. Egyptian Foreign Minister Amr Musa said the agreement would create new tensions in the Middle East, while the Iraqi press said the agreement would encourage Israel to continue its policy of occupation in the region. This set the platform for the Grapes of Wrath operation against Hizbullah in Lebanon who, according to Israel, had started their offensive attacks against Israel by Katyushas. Peres, in what many considered an attempt to show himself capable of making tough military decisions, authorized the bombing of Hizbullah guerrillas in the south of Lebanon to bring security to the Galilee, recasting himself as a hard man before the coming elections. However, this resulted in forcing some 400,000 Lebanese civilians out of their towns and villages, turning them into refugees. Jordan's Prime Minister at the time, Abdul Karim Kabariti, travelled to Israel to relay two messages: one to Ezer Weizman and another to Peres, urging them to end military actions and resume diplomacy, explaining the negative impact the operations were having on public support for peace and on the overall Arab community. However, the trip was in vain since the following day, Israel shelled a UN base in Qana killing over 100 refugees, giving Hizbullah a decisive moral victory. The International community condemned Israel for targeting civilians; and the entire Arab world was boiling with anger at Israel's treatment of the Lebanese people and disregard for Arab blood, leadership and people.[2] Shortly after this event, thousands of Jordanians took to the street to demonstrate against Israel's aggression while eleven members of the Lower House of Parliament called for the abrogation of the Jordanian–Israeli treaty and expulsion of Israel's ambassador to Jordan.

By authorizing the killing of Ayyash, suspending talks with Syria while threatening it with the Turkish–Israeli agreement and finally by operation Grapes of Wrath, Peres antagonized many in the peace camp in the Arab world, strengthening not only cries against further normalization but against the peace itself.

Therefore, even though Peres' competitor, Netanyahu, was as good as politically dead in the wake of Rabin's assassination (since shortly before the event, he had given an incendiary speech against Labour's peacemakers, especially Rabin, describing them as traitors, inflaming Israeli radicals), he was able to win the elections and become prime minister. The Israeli press reported rumours of King Hussein refusing to help boost Peres's chances of winning by turning down an invitation to meet Peres with Clinton in Washington and meeting, instead, his competitor on the eve of the elections. To King Hussein, Netanyahu's victory actually brought optimism. Despite the fact that Netanyahu was Likud's candidate, King Hussein was fully aware that a Knesset majority approved Jordan's peace with Israel, meaning it was a peace not between Labour and Jordan, but between Israel and Jordan. Netanyahu brought the hope of a new beginning whereas with Peres the prospects already looked gloomy. Peres lost, having succeeded at antagonizing most of the pro-peace camp in the Arab world while boosting the chances of Netanyahu at a time when he was almost politically dead. After all, Rabin's widow, Lea, refused to shake hands with Netanyahu when he offered his condolences; and, as reported by leading Israeli press editorials at the time, his own party members seriously debated replacing him with someone without 'Rabin's blood' on his hands. However, to his credit, Peres realized the importance of giving Palestinians a sense of autonomy and as such supported withdrawals from the Occupied Territories as planned (except from Hebron), a practice that became, after him, almost a thing of the past.

Regretfully, the election of Netanyahu did not bring the improved prospects as Jordan had hoped. Netanyahu's coming to power marked the end of pragmatism in favour of the assertion of ideological hard-line policies with roots in Revisionist Zionism. In his book *A Place Among the Nations: Israel and the World*, Netanyahu revealed the influence of Ze'ev Jabotinsky's teachings and those of his father (a historian who served as an adviser to Jabotinsky) on him. In the book, he argues that the Jews did not usurp land from the Arabs but the other way round; he also discusses the British mandate in Palestine in a chapter entitled 'The Betrayal'. Overall, he saw the world as mostly hostile to the State of Israel, hence the need for the latter to shape its fate by the sword. Thus, Netanyahu's guiding principles presented to Knesset during the vote of confidence debate on 16 June 1996, constituted a war on the Oslo framework (Barari 2004). His policy statements on peace, security and foreign relations indicated that his government was opposed to an independent Palestinian state, determined to consolidate the settlements and above all committed to sole Israeli sovereignty over a unified Jerusalem. Consequently, towards the end of September 1996, Israel opened the Hasmonean Tunnel in Jerusalem (located alongside Haram al-Sharif) soon after a visit of the Prime Minister's adviser, Dore Gold, to Jordan (where he met with King Hussein) thereby suggesting Jordanian knowledge and consent of the Israeli project. The new gate was a symbolic and psychological affront to the Palestinians and a violation of the pledge to resolve the issue of Jerusalem by negotiations. Arab leaders expressed their disappointment with Netanyahu and especially with King Hussein who had not joined in the earlier denunciation following his victory. The Arab leaders, so alarmed by Likud's victory, called a two-day summit in Cairo where Jordan was the only state to insist on continued normalization, arguing it was the only way to encourage Israel to move forward. King Hussein was well aware of the psychological dimension of the process and the need for confidence-building measures in order to foster and build peace. Indeed, his commitment to peace went far beyond words and his knowledge of the Israeli scene well exceeded that of many of his Arab peers. The summit was intended to restore Arab cohesion and sent a clear message to Israel and the United States that unless the new Israeli prime minister respected the foundations for peace established in the Madrid conference (i.e. the principle of land for peace), the peace process would collapse plunging the region in more tension and violence. Syria urged Arab states at this conference to contemplate other options than peace, including war, while President Mubarak stated that Arab countries would have to reconsider their positions if Israel assumed a hard-line position. Against this background, the Israeli act was even more embarrassing to the Jordanian leadership, placing it in an awkward position, domestically as well as regionally, and was in itself a direct violation of international norms and Jerusalem provisions in the peace treaty which called upon Israel not to seize, damage or change historic and religious buildings and sites. Violence in the West Bank and Gaza erupted with eighty Palestinians and fifteen Israeli soldiers dying in the clashes during which Palestinian police officers opened fire on their Israeli counterparts. Calls for abrogating the peace treaty again rose in Jordan from opposition parties. King Hussein, at a summit meeting in Washington, spoke angrily to Netanyahu of the 'arrogance of power' and warned that maintaining a fortress mentality would not bring around the peace that Israel wished.[3]

A welcome positive change emerged with Netanyahu and Arafat's signing of the Hebron Protocol. However, Netanyahu made up for his leniency by adopting a hard line on Jerusalem to appease internal opposition from his party. Announcing the plans for expanding the Jewish settlement housing in Har Homa (eastern part of Jerusalem known in Arabic as Jabal Abu Ghneim) came in spite of regional and international appeals to the contrary. This constituted another example in the Arab world of 'establishing facts on the ground' through illegitimate acquisition of land, an expansionist policy practised by Israel, shaking off the dust of the dominant ideological Arab frames and cognitive beliefs. History, it appeared, was repeating itself and lessons the Arabs should have learned seemed to be in need of a quick revision. In a letter to Netanyahu, King Hussein spoke of his concern over such actions and Israeli policies that would undermine and destroy accomplishments to date. He posed the question: 'How can I work with you as a partner and true friend in this confused and confusing atmosphere ... I have discovered that you have your own mindset and appear in no mood for any advice from a friend'.[4] Netanyahu's response placed the blame elsewhere, stating that he had 'inherited a process that was failing', making it clear that he remained committed to the expansion of settlement housing in East Jerusalem.[5] Exacerbation of Jordanian–Israeli relations took place a few days later with the killing of seven Israeli schoolgirls by a Jordanian soldier in al-Baqura, the area hailed, ironically enough, as the paradise of peace. The King, returning home immediately from a trip abroad, made his second visit to Jerusalem after the assassination of Rabin to offer personal condolences to the families of the victims in Israel.

By the end of September 1997, Jordan's relations with Israel reached their lowest point following the failed Mossad attempt against Khalid Mashal's life (Israel blamed him for the bombing of the Israeli embassy in Argentina in the early 1990s). Mossad decided to kill the chief of Hamas' political bureau in Amman by injecting a slow-acting poison into his ear. The plan was carried out, but Mashal was not killed. The plot caused much fury within Israel and the Arab parties. Israeli chief of staff and the director of military intelligence were unaware of the plan until they heard reports that two Mossad agents – disguised as Canadian tourists – had been apprehended by the Jordanian authorities in Amman. The Mossad agent in Amman is said to have been opposed to the operation for fear of damaging relations with Jordan, but the Prime Minister had given permission to proceed. King Hussein was livid with outrage (Shlaim 2001: 586) contemplating at the time a harsh retaliation. The Mossad attempt shocked him, discrediting his earlier assurances and claims that peace with Israel would enhance Jordan's security and ensure its territorial integrity. Furious, King Hussein gave Israel two options: were Mashal to die, the identity of the agents would be revealed and they would then be tried publicly and executed in Jordan; the second option was Israeli admittance of guilt, an apology and an antidote to the poison used (Barari 2004: 35–6). Netanyahu chose the latter and sent his chief of Mossad (Danny Yatom) to Amman with the antidote. Later, Netanyahu and his then Infrastructure Minister, Ariel Sharon, paid a quick visit to Jordan but the King refused to meet them. They met his brother, Crown Prince Hassan, instead. As a quid pro quo, they agreed to release Sheikh Ahmed Yassin, the spiritual leader and founder of Hamas in exchange for releasing the agents. Sheikh Ahmed Yassin was released, returned to Gaza via Amman, and the head of Mossad replaced in an attempt to mend fences with Jordan following this display of disregard to Jordan's leadership and its security, and a violation of article 4 of the treaty dealing with security.[6] Thereafter, interstate relations remained marred.

To his full credit, King Hussein never gave up hope to move forward with the peace process. He, therefore, sent a second letter to Netanyahu asking him to implement the second Israeli withdrawal from the West Bank warning of the dangers of a deadlock in the peace process to Jordan's own security and the region's security as a whole – but the king's appeal had little impact. Having broken the Likud taboo on handing over land for peace, Netanyahu adopted a hard-line position on Jerusalem to make up for singing the Hebron Protocol. He resisted any compromise or meaningful negotiations over Jerusalem, knowing very well that no Arab would accept less than what Arafat was demanding: shared sovereignty. As such, he commenced the work on a Jewish settlement in Har Homa (Jabal Abu Ghuneim) cutting off Jerusalem from the West Bank and strengthening Jewish hold over the city to better his negotiation position in any final negotiations. Concerning the West Bank, he offered the Palestinian National Authority 40 per cent while keeping 60 per cent for Israel, a proposition the Palestinians were bound to refuse, expecting no less than 90 per cent under the terms of the Interim Agreement of September 1995 known as Oslo II.

The United States' policy remained throughout opposed to acts of violence perpetrated by Palestinian Islamist groups, urging the PNA to take more serious action against the perpetrators than the 'revolving door' process of arrests and releases. Albright actually argued that confiscating land for building settlements could not be compared to killing people. While the statement is true, it reflects a poor understanding of the nature of the conflict and the significance attached by Arabs to the act of settlement-building and its tactical implications.

The policies of Netanyahu prompted more than 1,500 reserve officers and police force members, including 12 retired major generals to call on the prime minister to abandon his policy of expanding Jewish settlements in Palestinian areas and to choose peace instead. Their published letter to Netanyahu said that continued Israeli rule of 2.5 million Palestinians could harm the democratic and Jewish character of the state and made it difficult to identify with the government policies. 'A government that prefers maintaining settlements beyond the Green Line to solving the historic conflict and establishing normal relations in our region will cause us to question the righteousness of our path' the letter stated (Shlaim 2001: 587), exposing the conflict between the proponents of Greater Israel and the peace-camp who agreed to the land-for-peace formula.[7] In response, the Likud government started redrawing maps including what Ariel Sharon had coined the 'national interests' of the state to include Jewish settlements in the occupied territories. What is important to note here is that the government started blurring the distinction in the public's mind between vital *security needs* (as defined by the General Staff) *and national interests* as defined by its own right-wing ideology, which treated every Jewish settlement as sacrosanct. According to *Peace Now*,

Netanyahu had established 17 new hilltop settlements since the Wye Agreement, increasing the West Bank settler population by 40,000 Jews, making it difficult for any future Palestinian state to expand beyond the 29 per cent of the West Bank partially controlled by the PNA. At the same time, Netanyahu's credibility was further weakened by reneging on the international agreements entered into by his predecessors, as well as ones entered into by himself (e.g. Wye Agreement). He refused to implement this agreement (by handing over 5 per cent of the West Bank to the PNA for joint Israeli–Palestinian control) preferring to maintain exclusive Israeli control. Hamas's response was to blow up a car in Jerusalem killing the two Palestinian bombers and injuring 21 people.

The decision to hold new Israeli elections amounted to an admission by the Likud that Netanyahu had failed as a national leader and as prime minister. Barak (a security man, *betahonist,* and Israel's most decorated soldier) won, enjoying more credibility and trust as someone who would not 'sell out' on his people in dealing with the Arabs. Barak presented himself as the heir of Rabin, a soldier turned peacemaker, a soldier-statesman, not Peres, the poet-philosopher. To a public worried about security, Barak seemed to have the perfect combination.

The elections of 1999 in Israel deserve some elaboration in light of their uniqueness in the sense that for the first time ever, Arab journalists came to Israel to cover the event and interview candidates. The Qatar-based al-Jazeera satellite television station had full and detailed coverage of the campaign. Overall, there was a contrast with the historic Arab position that all Israelis were essentially alike in their evil nature. Ehud Barak and Yitzhak Mordechai were now seen as representing, more or less, the forces of good against Netanyahu.[8] The Arab world had to deal with Israel and realized that the choice of Prime Minister made a difference; therefore, more attention to differences between parties and policies became the norm. Apparently, the historic position and opinion that 'no difference between former prime ministers Menachem Begin and Yitzhak Rabin, or between Netanyahu and former prime minister Shimon Peres existed, have become obsolete and ineffective' (Bar'el 1999). In fact, Arab leaders and people were looking to the voting and public opinion poll in Israel as an indicator of Israeli public opinion on the peace process and, as such, the elections became a confidence-building measure from Palestinian and Arab perspectives.

While the Palestinian leadership originally said elections were an internal Israeli affair in which they had no business interfering, shortly before the elections, enthusiastic PNA figures were urging Israelis to 'vote for peace', blaming the stalemate in the peace process on Netanyahu's government (Rubin 1999). The Egyptian press echoed the same sentiment by concluding that Israelis would not vote for Netanyahu knowing how damaging his policies were (ibid.). Indeed, the overall mood in the Arab world was against Netanyahu's re-election. In the words of Mahmoud Murad, 'while Arabs had no preference on either candidate, they simply hated Netanyahu' (*al-Akhbar*, 16 May 1999). Salah Bassiouny, a former diplomat heading the Cairo Peace Movement said 'Our experience with Netan-yahu is bitter and very disappointing' (*Jerusalem Post*, 5 February 1999), a feeling echoed by the Jordanian editor, Hasanat who said that Netanyahu's ideology stopped him from making a territorial compromise concluding that 'in many ways, you feel that he looks down at Arabs and this is what we don't like' (ibid.).

Needless to say, the Arab radical opposition's views were different, faithful to the traditional slogan of no difference between one Israeli government or another, reminding people that most Arab–Israeli wars were waged under Labour-led governments.

In the same line of thought, the Palestinian National Authority's Information Ministry said that Israeli candidates were depicting Palestinians as 'savage terrorists' with candidates competing to show which Israeli killed the largest number of them and as such deserves a larger number of votes (Rubin 1999). Nonetheless, the Palestinians remained, naturally, very interested in the elections as their partner in the process was being selected. After the deadlock in negotiations and implementation of reached agreements under Netanyahu, PNA officials and Arab leaders were eager for a positive change in the form of a Labour-led government. There was a realization that the Palestinian National Authority could play a favourable role in influencing the elections in Barak's favour. In fact, it was a key consideration when deciding not to unilaterally declare Palestinian independence on the fifth anniversary of the agreement signed in Cairo on 4 May 1994 implementing the Oslo accords. Such a declaration would, most likely, have swung Israeli public opinion more in favour of the hard-line policies of Likud, which prompted the peace camp in Israel, especially Yossi Beilin, to ask Arafat to postpone such a declaration lest Barak's chances at victory be ruined (Rubin 1999). Other factors dissuading Arafat from making the declaration were warnings from the European Union and the United States against such a move, which meant that compliance would secure backing and benefits in the future. Above all, Arafat realized that such a verbal declaration, if not made with enough support and backing, would be meaningless and might in fact cause more damage than benefit if Israel decided to respond aggressively, stopping the peace process or, worse, annexing the West Bank territory altogether (Rubin 1999). While Hamas claimed absence of an agreement with the Palestinian National Authority to halt violence during elections time so as not to push Israeli voters towards more hard-line positions, no violence increase was evident either, which was also true of Hizbullah's activities (ibid.).

However, the victory of Barak did not halt the deterioration along the Israeli–Palestinian peace track. Barak would later repeat the statement that he was the only prime minister who had not transferred land to the Palestinians, making his position at odds with his party's policy of land for peace and undermining the Palestinians' faith in his sincerity to proceed with the peace process (Pundak 2001). This suspicion grew when he refused to transfer control of three villages on the outskirts of Jerusalem (Abu Dis, Al Eyzaria, and Arab Sawahra) to the PNA, even after Knesset approval of the transfer (Pundak 2001: 34). Barak did not try to establish a good working relationship with Arafat in spite of the poor relations between the disputing parties following Netanyahu's premiership. Instead of initiating a meeting with Arafat, who was expecting one (in the hope it would serve as a confidence-building measure reassuring the Palestinians of the continuity of the peace process and alleviating some of the pressures and burdens on the PNA), Barak refused to meet Arafat one-on-one during the two-week long talks at Camp David – even when Arafat repeatedly requested such a meeting. This came in sharp contrast with Rabin and Peres who each had his own working relationship with Arafat which acted as a safety net during times of crisis. Under the circumstances, the Palestinian leader was even quoted as saying 'Barak is worse than Netanyahu' (Pundak 2001: 38).

Although Barak announced that no new settlements would be established, when settlers began constructing hilltop strongholds illegally he missed the chance of sending both Israelis and Palestinians a clear message of support to the peace process by removing the strongholds through legal means, given that the Palestinians considered them to be new settlements. Perhaps being 'emotionally sympathetic to Gush Emunim, the settlers' movement and mentally conditioned by his 35 years in the military' were reasons for his inaction (Pundak 2001: 37). Rationally, though, Barak was left-wing. He understood that peace required relinquishing land occupied in 1967. He understood that the occupation was doing both the Israelis and Palestinians much damage, but his actions contradicted his rational analyses. He was probably still unconvinced that the Palestinian leadership made the shift in paradigm from total destruction of the Jewish state to living peacefully by its side. With such a mindset, he presented his deal at the final-status negotiations as 'peace by ultimatum',[9] which along with his insistence on closure did not create a congenial context for bargaining (Arafat's historic mistake, however, was not accepting it or at least coming up with a counter proposal).

The countdown to violence began with the collapse of the Camp David Summit. The spark was the visit of Ariel Sharon to al Haram al Sharif (Temple Mount) on 28 September 2000. The visit was perceived by many as part of an attempt to change the religious status quo in the area of the noble sanctuary by building a Jewish synagogue within the boundaries of the sacred compound, an act not contemplated since the destruction of the Temple in AD 70. This fuelled a wave of anger and fury among Palestinians and Muslims in the Arab world as it constituted another attempt at the familiar policy of establishing facts on the ground to boost the Israeli negotiation position, bringing a breakdown in the permanent-status negotiations. Above all, the act revived the Intifada with one major difference: this time, it was under the leadership of Fatah, not Hamas.

Since September 2000, the peace process has been in a state of collapse with the second Palestinian Intifada shaking both communities. The Palestinians thought Israelis were unwilling or ready to pay the price of peace in land, greatly underestimating the impact the Islamist attacks and bombings had on deepening the polarization within the Israeli society and weakening the peace constituency. Economic hardships, again, played their expected role in mounting Palestinian frustrations as the 'fruits of peace' grew more elusive to the average Palestinian person. Closures prevented the injection of an essential flow of funds to the

Palestinian economy, which, along with restrictions on movement, served as collective punishment. Other day-to-day frustrations included a permit-issuing system for travel, which mainly hurt those who already had been cleared by Israeli security. Topped with a dramatic decrease in employment opportunities in Israel, new pockets of poverty emerged.

Frustration on the Palestinian side led the Fatah and the Tanzim (the local organization base of Fatah) to lead the second Intifada. Since they upheld the Oslo process and the 'liberation of land' through a just peace, they had paved the way for the process ensuring local support, taking moral responsibility for it. Once their expectations failed to materialize, 'they felt they bore the responsibility for a barren process and even an historical trap' (Pundak 2001: 44). Therefore, Fatah preferred to lead the uprising as opposed to wait for Hamas to lead them into an uprising.

In an effort to get the peace process back on track, Clinton convened the parties at the White House on 23 December 2000 and presented to them 'The Clinton Parameters'. These envisaged an independent Palestinian state over the whole of Gaza and 94–6 per cent of the West Bank with East Jerusalem as capital. These were the bases for negotiations between the Israeli and Palestinian teams at Taba in January 2001 when the two parties came closer than ever before to reaching a final status agreement; but time ran out on them with the elections on 6 February 2001 bringing Ariel Sharon into the premiership. Sharon immediately renounced the Taba understandings, and the change in Washington's administration headed by George W. Bush made it possible for the latter to renounce the Clinton Parameters as gone with the outgoing administration. Deterioration along the Palestinian–Israeli track continued, especially with the siege of Arafat and the reoccupation of Ramallah and other Palestinian cities, prompting King Abdullah in March 2002 to request the dispatching of international peacekeepers to protect the Palestinian civilians. At the same time, Jordan's then foreign minister, Dr. Marwan Muasher, summoned Israel's ambassador to Jordan, David Dadonn, and protested Israel's 'irresponsible actions'. The immediate repercussions in Jordan were angry people taking to the streets in protest.

In June 2002, President Bush shared his vision on how the conflict should be resolved, meeting with the Israeli and Palestinian prime ministers in the city of Aqaba to the South of Jordan. However, the vision did not produce the hoped-for results. It built on the premise that until the Palestinians changed their leadership and underwent far-reaching reforms in terms of security performance and governance, the international community's help and support in the process would not be made available. While the Palestinians were required to proceed with the reform, fewer requirements were made, at the time, of the Israelis.[10] The agreement triggered violent attacks, plunging both parties in a familiar vicious cycle of bloodshed that put an end to the proposed vision.

Again, another effort was made to revive the peace process with Tony Blair's 'Roadmap' which everybody supported: the United States, Britain, the fifteen members of the European Union and Russia. They all agreed on the need to end the conflict in the region following the invasion of Iraq. The 'Roadmap', launched in May 2003, basically envisaged three phases leading to an independent Palestinian state alongside Israel by 2005. The Palestinians embraced it; Sharon, however, submitted fourteen amendments that undermined any serious political content. The Israeli cabinet never endorsed the Roadmap and only voted for specific measures that were required of Israel in the first phase. The policies of the Israeli government therefore did not change because of the Roadmap: Israel continued its incursions into Palestinian areas, assassinations of Palestinian militants and leadership figures (including Sheikh Ahmad Yassin, founder of Hamas and its spiritual leader, killed on 22 March 2004), demolition of houses, uprooting of trees and imposing curfews. These were all perceived as deliberate infliction of misery to encourage the transfer of Palestinians outside the Occupied Territories, a threatening prospect for Jordan whose government made these fears known to Sharon.

Jordan saw the building of the separation wall as another threat to its own security since it encouraged influx immigration into Jordan. Consequently, this was a primary reason why Jordan led the opposition to the wall in the Arab World, presenting its case before the Court in Hague, obtaining a ruling that the wall (as well as Israeli annexation of territories occupied in 1967) were illegal. The political relations between Israel and Jordan were tense, with the Embassy in Tel Aviv functioning without an Ambassador since the resumption of violence in 2000.

Overcoming obstacles: the cases of water and the economy

Despite the backdrop of continued deterioration explained earlier, serious efforts were made at top-level political leadership in both states to overcome obstacles facing implementation of key agreements. This was true of the thorny issues of borders and security, which were resolved to mutual satisfaction, as well as water rights and economic cooperation prospects.

Water Rights

The water agreement dealt with water issues through articles dedicated to matters of allocation, storage, water quality and protection, groundwater in Wadi Araba, notification and agreement, cooperation and a joint water committee.[11] Mainly, Jordan obtained most of its dues under agreement with Israel.

Economic Cooperation

Article 7 of the Treaty of Peace stipulated that within six months of exchanging the ratification letters, negotiations on economic and trade matters should be concluded. The Trade and Economic Cooperation Agreement was finished and signed exactly one year later, on 25 October 1995. Since it took six months for the agreement to be ratified, it went into operation on 19 April 1996. Obstacles emerged with the signing of the agreement. The first was related to the issue of border crossing. The agreement called for a back-to-back mode of transport whereby goods are to reach the border, be unloaded, inspected (for security reasons) and then loaded onto Israeli trucks with access to the market. To Jordanian exporters, the system proved ineffective, costly and restrictive, given that a ceiling on truck numbers was established (limiting the flow of goods) and that certain days of the week (Saturday and Sunday) are weekend days in Israel on which no business could be conducted. The second problem involved strict rules and regulations on standards and specifications at both content and administration levels. This was compounded by absence of set rules of accreditation between the two countries. Jordan's accreditation was not accepted in Israel; therefore, the latter would test items from Jordan such as foodstuff, chemicals and electronic devices, taking months to conduct the research and produce results. Another obstacle was related to tariffs. Unforeseen tariffs were imposed on Jordanian exports, thereby reducing the margin of profit to be gained from comparatively low production costs. The Israelis demanded custom tariff, other internal tariffs like VAT, purchase tax and TAMA. While the application of internal taxes was possible in the absence of preferential treatment stipulated in the bilateral agreement, the TAMA tax in particular is a mark-up to the custom tariff, widely believed to be used when the Israeli authorities feel that custom tariff is not enough to prohibit competition with the local production. Originally, given that Israel's GNP is at least 11 times greater than that of Jordan, no tariffs were to be imposed on the movement of goods from Jordan to Israel and the PNA in an attempt to bridge the large gap between the two countries' economies (Rubenstein 1996: 563). Therefore, Jordanians saw in this tax situation an attempt to monopolize the Palestinian markets.[12] Not surprisingly, the available official statistics from the Jordanian customs department showed that Jordanian exports in 1998 amounted to US$23 million (a mere 1 per cent of Israeli exports to the Territories which in 1998 went over US$2 billion). Leading Jordanian business managers blamed Israeli intransigence and monopoly over Palestinian markets for discouraging Jordanian business groups from embarking on economic relations with Israel, giving them no incentive to defy the rejectionist domestic front.[13] Furthermore, they complained of difficulties obtaining visas to conduct business in Israel.[14]

Given the mounting frustration among those Jordanians willing to do business with Israel, the latter collaborated with Jordan to resolve these issues. A reconsideration of the trade protocol was finalized to Jordan's satisfaction on 4 December 1996. The main reconsideration was an adjustment of customs tariffs. A second major development was a reconsideration of the transport agreement between the two countries as of 1 January 1997 whereby the back-to-back system was changed into a point-to-door system. The system came about as a result of Jordanian complaints of the delays and increased costs resulting from the back-to-back system. The amendment, Jordanian officials argued, had a positive impact on trade relations. As to the difficulties facing trade between the two countries, mainly due to the application of Israeli standards on Jordanian exports, the two parties signed an agreement laying the ground rules for mutual recognition of certifications, marks of conformity, standards procedures, fees for services rendered, accreditation of laboratories and other issues including confidentiality and liability. Concerning the problems of obtaining visas, the Israeli Embassy made it common practice to issue invitation letters to business persons applying for visas with which they would skip the long queues and stand in special, much shorter ones.

Jordanians realized that the Israeli market, despite its openness to the world and WTO accession and other free trade areas such as NAFTA and EFTA, remained a closed economy and highly protected against outside competition, especially in the newly captured markets in the West Bank and Gaza. These formed the second largest export market for Israeli products with a volume of more than US$2.5 billion a year. Therefore, joint ventures to enter the United States markets were proposed to remedy the situation, hence the signing of the Jordan–Israel agreement on the Irbid Qualified Industrial Zone (QIZ). Qualified industrial zones are a special form of extraterritorial economic arrangements whose exports to the US are tariff-free by US decree. QIZs exist in Jordan upon an amendment introduced to the US–Israel Free Trade Area Implementation Act of 1985, introduced into the US House of Representatives and signed into law in 1996, granting the US president additional proclamation authority to extend the US–Israel free trade area to include products from QIZ between Israel and Jordan. The rationale of this legislation is that the production of tangible economic benefits would broaden the support base for the peace process. The QIZ offers duty and quota-free access to the US market for products manufactured by the 'qualified' enterprises located in enclaves designated by the United Sates Trade Representatives as QIZ. Of particular benefit is the fact that no requirement for any reciprocal benefit is required on behalf of the QIZ hosting country.

The agreement (based on the US–Israel Free Trade Area of 1985 and the US president's proclamation No. 6955) was signed in Doha, Qatar in 1997. However, an indication of good trade levels is not merely dependent on figures issued by the Jordanian department of statistics on the matter since these do not necessarily include joint ventures operating under a company name registered in Europe (which is the case with a large number of joint ventures operating in the QIZs).

Products manufactured in the QIZs are subject to 35 per cent minimum QIZ content, which means that at least one third (11.7 per cent) must be added by the Jordanian manufacturer in the QIZ and another third by an Israeli manufacturer, reduced to eight per cent and seven per cent in high-tech products for a period of five years (as of February 1999). The remainder of the 35 per cent content may be fulfilled by production in the QIZ, the West Bank, Gaza, Israel or the US.

The nature of the agreement addressed many of the issues that served as obstacles in the face of Jordanian trade with Israel, namely problems related to import restrictions, protectionist standards, testing, labelling and certification requirements as well as various banking, securities and insurance-related concerns. They also open new non-conventional markets for Jordanian exports, thus helping to upgrade the quality of the products. That is, although the heaviest investment was initially textile-related and the manufacture of clothing (including jeans, sportswear and luggage destined for major US retail chains), a change took place in early 2001 when jewellery manufacturing was introduced along with an exporter to operate in the Cyber City QIZ. This represents a major attempt at diversification from traditional products. Located next to the Jordan University for Science and Technology in Irbid the city, when completed, is expected to have approximately 500 tenants with a working population of 200,000. QIZs will attract direct foreign investment to the zones as well as technology transfer and job creation opportunities and training of local employees at the hands of skilled labourers. The United States Embassy in Amman privately estimated the figure of Jordanian workers in QIZs in November 2001 to be up to 14,000 while towards the end of 2003 private estimates claimed that the figure was close to 20,000 with most jobs going to women (Khasawneh and Khouri 2002: 23). The job creation opportunities have not been paralleled by any other industry in the Kingdom (for example, jobs went from 6,000 in 2000 to 11,000 at the end of August 2001), an admirable accomplishment given the scale of unemployment in Jordan. The added importance of these fast-growing job opportunities is that they are offered in parts of Jordan that suffer from heavy unemployment. This helps to curb the rural–urban migration and eases the pressure on Amman and major cities. In its job creation opportunities, QIZ far outweigh those offered at any time by the traditional Free Zones.[15] Above all, they generate foreign currencies that build up the country's reserves through increased exports. Exports in 1999, about US$2.4 million of QIZ products, went up drastically. For example, exports from the end of April in 2001 to the end of August in the same year went up to US$50 million. Another indication of expansion is the growing number of companies from 27 to 30 with five more applying for qualifying status, all during the same period. In addition, many Asian garment companies moved from Dubai to avoid US quotas. The QIZ experience enhances the importance of the private sector in the wake of the government's policy for privatization launched in the 1990s and 2000s.

In short, the QIZ experience is hailed as a success story for Jordan, a phenomenon witnessing rapid growth and expansion all over the country, thereby serving as a tangible peace dividend.[16] The QIZ would hardly have come about had it not been for the peace treaty Jordan signed with Israel, which enabled the execution of the idea. Egypt and the Occupied Territories are believed to benefit from a similar QIZ experience – especially in light of possible US legislation allowing for it – and the needed employment opportunities it could generate in these countries. In evaluating the QIZ experience, Jordan compared it with its free zones initiatives. The US–Jordan Free Trade Agreement (FTA) was signed on 24 October 2000 and ratified on 24 September 2001 (but preceded by the QIZ Agreement). The agreement was the first between the United States and an Arab country and the fourth signed by the United States after similar deals with Canada, Israel and Mexico. Jordan was familiar with Free Zone (FZ) arrangements as these areas exist within its boundaries. However, these zones have not proved to be particularly beneficial to the economy. In terms of employment and the qualitative aspect of the jobs they generate, results have not been impressive (Khasawneh and Khouri 2002). This comes in sharp contrast with the QIZs' employment creation achievements. In terms of types of jobs created by the QIZs, technologies and training offered, they are indeed superior to the Free Zone's success. Therefore, Jordan considers the QIZ experience a success story that could be replicated in other Arab countries, especially Egypt and the West Bank. Jordanian officials stress the accomplishments of Jordan, highlighting its exports to the US that rose from less than US$20 million in 1999 to over US$200 million by 2002 (Moore 2003). More than 20,000 jobs have been created in the QIZs with reported 70 per cent going to women.

Conclusion

Tracing the progress in the Jordanian–Israeli relations between 1994 and 2003 shows that consolidating the peace was the Jordanian top-level leadership's primary concern after signing the treaty with Israel and that doing so was challenging given the continuous deterioration in relations between the two states following the assassination of Israeli Prime Minister Yitzhak Rabin. From a Jordanian viewpoint, relations embarked on a nosedive because of Israeli policies not only as far as Jordan was concerned but also with other Arab parties (e.g. Syria and Lebanon), particularly Palestinian relations.

The discussion in this chapter indicates that overall, Israel perceived its peace track with the Palestinians to be detached and separate from the Jordanian one. With Jordan, there was much progress (albeit at some levels more than others), with the Palestinians, however, there was continuous breakdown at all levels. The coming chapters will indicate that the Israeli assumption of detachment between the two tracks was flawed as the breakdown in the peace process with the Palestinians had a tremendous effect on the type of peace Jordan ended up having with Israel, its popularity and degree of 'warmth'.

4 Obstacles to a warm peace at the structural level[1]

While the previous chapter displayed the efforts of the political elite in paving the way, especially as far as policies are concerned, for normalization, this chapter and the next one will examine the obstacles to a 'warm peace'. Both chapters will argue that obstacles at the levels of structure and agency steered the process away from the path originally intended by the top-level political leaderships. In particular, it will discuss the structural obstacles to a warm peace, examining the political and economic relations, albeit from a Jordanian viewpoint. It will argue that notwithstanding the Jordanian leadership's hopes for a warm peace, existing and emerging obstacles in these spheres made it difficult to move beyond the state of formal peace and to build a 'warm' one.

The socio-political dimension

At the interstate level, relations grew cold after the death of Rabin and continued to deteriorate seriously with Netanyahu in power, a state of affairs that continued with the resumption of the second Intifada, under Barak, and the subsequent building of the separation wall by the Likud-led government of Ariel Sharon. Given Jordan's demographic make-up, a key factor affecting the relations between both states was the continuous deadlock in the peace talks between the PLO/PNA and Israel, contradicting the general Israeli understanding of the detachment of both peace tracks. Of particular interest was the role played by the escalating violence in the Occupied Territories in arousing public sympathy, consolidating popular anti-Israeli frames in Jordan and validating distrustful interpretive schemes. Consequently, it became more and more difficult to speak of normalization.

Violence in the Occupied Territories

On 4 June 2003, a high-profile summit took place at the Jordanian Red Sea Resort of Aqaba between the Israeli Prime Minister Ariel Sharon and his Palestinian counterpart Mahmoud Abbas under the auspices of George W. Bush to launch the latest Middle East peace initiative. To emphasize that no initiative could be implemented without the armed factions, al-Aqsa Martyrs' Brigades of Fatah, the Izz Eddin Al Qassam Brigades of Hamas and Islamic Jihad's Jerusalem Battalions conducted an unprecedented combined attack on the Erez junction between Israel and Gaza leaving four soldiers dead. Escalation on both sides reached dramatic proportions when, following the failed Israeli attempt to assassinate the political leader of Hamas, Abd al Aziz Rantisi, in Gaza on 10 June, a series of killings by Palestinian militants ensued along with retaliatory Israeli helicopter attacks. These left some 50 dead, almost all civilians, and hundreds wounded (Rabbani 2003).

However, the cycle of violence had started much earlier in the process, mainly in response to the exclusion of paramilitary groups from the process (not to mention its secrecy). These groups' understanding that the Oslo agreements were in essence a Palestinian renouncement of the resistance based on a promise of an end to the occupation and some form of autonomy (not independence), while Israel continued to have a monopoly over water, land and security resources with continued settlement building.[2] Aggravating matters was the fact that the ideological base of most of these militant groups did not favour peace within a two-state scenario.

As a reaction to the peace process, Islamic Jihad began its attacks against Israel in 1995 killing 19 Israelis in Beit Lid, resulting in Israel sealing off the Occupied Territories. The Islamists continued their attacks which, while undermining the structures upon which the foundations for peace were being erected, did not deter the resolution of the 1994 Nobel Peace prize laureates (Arafat, Peres and Rabin) from their goal of pursuing peace. In fact, so undeterred were the peacemakers that they signed the Oslo II accords providing for the extension of autonomy of the West Bank. Response, however, came from another side: Israel's war hero and peacemaker Yitzhak Rabin was assassinated in 1995 by Yigal Amir, an Israeli right-wing extremist.

In 1996, Arafat won the elections and became the president of the Palestinian National Authority but Hamas resumed its offensives in Jerusalem, Tel Aviv and Ashkelon. Not surprisingly, Israel's elections in 1996 were won by the right-wing coalition led by Benyamin Netanyahu. Labour's agenda for the elections in 1996 was to oppose the building of new settlements and to encourage a solution to the Israeli–Palestinian problem within a 'Jordanian–Palestinian framework'. Labour also deliberately dropped from their platform the reference to the Golan Heights as a 'strategic asset' for Israel and replaced it with 'nationally important region to the State of Israel' (Rabbani 2003: 3). The 'land for peace' approach of Labour and the 'Not one Inch' of Likud led to the polarization of the Israeli people regarding the issue of peace with the Palestinians and other Arab countries like Syria. In light of recent repeated attacks against Israel and the seemingly too fast a pace for the Israelis, polarization in Israel shifted towards the harder line of the right wing.

One has to remember that Likud and Labour are not parties in the traditional sense of the word, but rather political blocs dependent upon different coalitions made up of different parties, some of which emerge only to disintegrate before the next elections; therefore, the coalition formation is very indicative of the popular views concerning the peace process. While both Likud and Labour converged on the issue of recognition, they diverged on territorial compromise. Labour called for the adjustment of Israel to the pre-1967 borders as a condition to accommodating Israel's security requirements. Therefore, it had no problem adhering to these principles especially when the agreements stressed the need for gradual approach in implementation, meaning gradual redeployment of Israeli forces on the West Bank as the PNA assumed the required responsibilities on both political and security issues in agreed-upon areas. Likud, however, sought to ignore the entire Oslo process in favour of final status talks without much preludes or preparatory steps; it mainly adopted a policy of 'not an inch'. The wide gap between the political agendas of the two leading parties and the significant difference in their ideological and political platforms then was a key reason why decisions taken by a Labour government to push the peace process forward were not supported by a subsequent government led by the Likud. For example, when the Labour-led government took power in 1992, it prohibited construction of any new settlements (but allowed construction to continue on ones already being built). In fact, with the exception of the Jerusalem area, no new construction was permitted under this government. Although Labour considered Har Homa/Jabal Abu Ghneim to be part of Jerusalem's southern municipal areas, it deliberately did not allow any construction to take place there until final status talks established the final boundaries for all of Jerusalem. This was the policy between 1992 and 1996. However, when the Likud coalition took over, Prime Minister Netanyahu declared himself, on 17 October 1996, personally responsible for advancing the new government's settlement expansion programme. Not surprisingly, he initiated the programme for the development of Har Homa despite the political ramifications of the act. Taking into account the importance of the issue of settlements to the Palestinians and its relevance to the Oslo agreements, such significant shifts in position from one government to another were bound to have negative impacts on the entire process and further validate the Islamists' preference for continued violence, especially by Hamas[3] and Islamic Jihad. As a competitor for the PLO, Hamas mounted bitter criticism against the PLO and took the liberty of organizing its own strikes and published its own covenant, constantly challenging 'PLO's claim to be the sole, legitimate representative of the Palestinian people'. Along with Islamic Jihad,[4] they are the strongest two religious parties. Many factors contributed to the mounting strength of Hamas, most important of which were Saudi subsidies during the Gulf War. This meant that, for a change, considerable funding was going to other parties than just the PLO. The large network it operated within and valuable social work it provided secured it 20 per cent of the Palestinian votes despite the PNA's pressure. Needless to say, the PLO was not successful at marginalizing Hamas as indicated by the November 1990 agreement in which Fatah acknowledged Hamas's right to have its own strikes and separate political activity.

How did the PLO handle Hamas?

The PLO's response to Hamas's mounting popularity was along three paths: a policy of co-option, managing a bitter polemic against it and using Hamas's internal strife against it. Arafat used the fissure between Hamas's military and political wings, for example, in 1995, holding dialogues with the political wing, seeking its participation in the political process while combating Izz Eddin Al Qassam brigades, overall weakening Hamas's resolve leading to a low-key participation in the elections. Furthermore, when the military wing of Hamas carried out attacks on Israel two months later, the acts received criticism from Islamist politicians. While these tactics may have proved successful in maintaining internal cohesion, to Israel, they were viewed as evidence of the presumed lack of real commitment by the Palestinian National Authority (PNA) to the peace process, even arguing that both were two sides of the same coin. Louis René Beres[5] viewed PLO/Hamas as playing the 'good-cop-bad-cop' routine and argued that whether deliberately or not, the way they worked suggested that they complimented each other.

To Israel, this defeated one of its greatest ambitions from the peace process with the Palestinians, namely to put an end to the attacks mounted against it by various Palestinian factions and groups, especially Hamas. It believed that the PLO would actually be able to prevent such attacks, which is why the Oslo accords contain a pledge by Yasser Arafat to prevent them. In the optimistic words of then-foreign minister, Shimon Peres, 'Why should we chase Hamas when the PLO can do it for us?'.[6] Oslo II reaffirmed that role of the PLO through its governing arm: the Palestinian National Authority. Doubts, however, exist on the Israeli side whether this role of the PLO was seriously engaged in at all. In essence, Israel was expecting the PLO to play the role of the Israeli Defence Forces in curbing violence.

From an Israeli point of view, success at counteracting Islamist attacks would be attested by the disarmament of militant groups, extradition of those requested by Israel for suspicion of direct involvement in attacks against it and the PLO's regard of such groups as Hamas and Islamic Jihad as enemies of the PNA as well. Concerning disarmament, Israel found the PLO very reluctant to affect a thorough decommissioning process in territories under its control with all Palestinian attempts at public crackdowns on Islamist militants being the result of mounting pressures to react following attacks made on Israel. Although the PNA announced two major crackdowns (the first was between September 1993 and April 1995, and the second in March 1996), both failed to yield much by way of results. For example, the PNA ordered all citizens in Gaza and Jericho possessing weapons to surrender them by 11 May 1995 in order to avoid having their weapons confiscated. The *New York Times*, however, noted that the deadline came and went without any visible response from the PLO-PNA (Klein 2003). When questioned about the lack of reaction from the police's side, Nasir Yusef, PLO-PNA police commander said nothing was done because Arafat did not give any orders for reaction (ibid.). Again, in March 1996, Arafat announced the intention of his forces to seize all illegal weapons in territories under PLO control. As a result, PNA police displayed, at a press conference held a few days later, some 50 pistols and an equal number of rifles they said were seized from Hamas members. The number was extremely low by comparison to what Hamas was estimated to have at its disposal. Israel also took issue with declarations made by Palestinian leaders like Farouq Qaddumi that 'no one can complain about what Hamas and Jihad are doing. I say it is the right of every Palestinian to struggle as long as there is a single Israeli soldier in the land of Palestine'. Israelis considered these validations of their conviction that no serious efforts at disarmament were carried out. After all, Arafat once publicly declared that the Palestinian Authority 'will not disarm Hamas'.

As to extradition, Israel always had an issue with the PLO over not extraditing persons it believed to be involved in attacks against it. PLO officials, allegedly, urged Muhammad Diaf (and other Hamas members) to flee the area and head to Sudan for temporary refuge. Arrests made by the PNA of Hamas and/or Jihad activists generally failed to satisfy Israel, since they usually targeted lower-level members whose arrest did not particularly bear much significance, especially as most of the arrested persons were quietly released afterwards. Furthermore, Arafat appeared in no hurry to arrest anyone responsible for the Iranian–Palestinian arms deal. Israel captured a ship in the Red Sea carrying arms and weapons from Iran to the Palestinians and demanded Palestinian enquiry and action, in absence of which Israel retaliated by reoccupying Rafah and destroying the Gaza airport.[7] Arafat denied knowledge of any kind of the deal.

The fact that the PLO's leadership sometimes blamed Israel for the attacks against Israelis (e.g. Arafat's remarks during the visit of Cardinal Bernardin of Chicago that Israeli nationalists were mounting the recent attacks to kill the peace process), while showing public deference to many key Hamas leaders highly sought by Israel, did very little to convince the Israelis that the PLO-PNA considered the attacks mounted by armed groups against Israel as a threat to the entire peace process and not just to Israel. If anything, these declarations seemed to strengthen Israeli right-wing beliefs that the second phase to the establishment of a Palestinian state would be the Palestinians' liquidation of the state of Israel itself. This belief was validated each time Arafat reconfirmed his loyalty to the refugees' right of return which, after all, was not compatible with a two-state solution. Indeed, the mainstream Israeli view held that an independent Palestinian state next door was more and more a prospect to be avoided if radical Arab streams were to be denied easy access into Israel. In short, while the PLO-PNA policy of co-option may have served it well in maintaining its control over such volatile areas as the West Bank and Gaza Strip, it did very little to convince its partner in the negotiations of its commitment to a common, peaceful future.

Moreover, the Israeli point of view even supported an argument to the effect that Hamas acted with the consent of the PLO – against whom it never mounted anything beyond a verbal attack – to balance the power asymmetries. Israelis were so convinced of the deliberate lenient treatment by the PLO of Hamas and Islamic Jihad that in 1998, the Wye River memorandum offered 13 per cent of the West Bank to the PNA as an incentive in exchange for stepping up Palestinian police repression of violent attacks against Israel. The Palestinian anti-terrorism plan was to be monitored by the CIA.[8] However, violence continued on both sides, with the Palestinian attacks usually targeting Israeli buses, resulting in casualties among soldiers and civilians. The attacks would entail harsh Israeli retaliations in the form of military incursions (including the six-hour raid on the Palestinian leadership's compound in Ramallah), reoccupation of areas from where it had earlier withdrawn (e.g. Rafah) as well as assassination of Islamist figures, especially among Hamas.[9] The cycle of attacks and counter-attacks prompted the UN Security Council to adopt resolution 1397 demanding 'immediate cessation of all acts of violence, including all acts of terror, provocation, incitement, and destruction' and resolution 1420 urging parties to 'move immediately to a meaningful ceasefire'. Throughout, the PLO/PNA was in a critical position since any claims it would make to not being able to curb the violence would serve the counter argument that it was incapable in the first place of assuming control of areas under its rule even if it wanted to. Therefore, the opposing argument that it depended on violence to address the asymmetry of powers involved in the conflict found more resonance. In the end, Israeli and United States' leaders bluntly stated their wish for Arafat to step down in favour of someone else, making the end of violence a precondition to resuming peace talks. Israel declared Arafat an unsuitable partner for negotiations and confined him to his headquarters in Ramallah, a place he only left for treatment in Paris from where his body was returned for burial in Ramallah in November 2004.

It is important to stress that the accuracy of this Israeli perception is not the main issue. More important was the cognitive belief that such actions were, to Israel, not in line with a serious commitment to the peace process. Overall, there was an Israeli disappointment with Oslo. It seemed to have paved the way for territorial concessions which, once seized by the Palestinians, became safe havens for extremist groups who would launch attacks disrupting the daily existence of Israelis, shredding to pieces any sense of security and peace the process promised to bring. The general belief among Israelis was that they gave up territories and made concessions for no peace at all; in fact, the continued violence made a very large portion of those in the Israeli peace camp wonder whether indeed Arafat and his authority were ever serious about a two-state solution as opposed to the full liquidation of the State of Israel,[10] especially when Barak in 2000 (and later Clinton in 2001), made offers many thought were 'generous' and yet rejected by Arafat. In conclusion, though the Israeli right lacked the energy and chances to stop the Oslo agreements, the suicide attacks energized them and their relentless commitment to the Land of Israel, vindicating their professed distrust of the PLO and the PNA (as quoted in Aggestam 1999: 168).

On the other side, the Palestinians also saw Israel as not seriously committed to peace. In addition to the controversial policies of settlement building and expansion, the closure of Palestinian enclaves resulted in a serious drop in living standards plunging the population into economic despair despite the signed accord's emphasis on the need for economic cooperation and development to improve the living conditions in the Occupied Territories. The end of 2003 marked more than a decade into the Oslo agreement and still no Palestinian state on the ground or the prospect of one looming on the horizon. Oslo came to be seen as a process at which the Palestinians gave up the right to resist the occupation for an elusive Israeli promise to end it. Not only did the occupation continue, but also settlement-building, demolition of houses and uprooting of trees. Concerning withdrawals, Israel had the upper hand, deciding when, where and how it would withdraw – if at all – from territories under its control. Absence of an international monitoring body to ensure compliance with mutual agreements gave Israel the right to continue acting as an occupation force. Towards the end of 2003, Israel started to implement a unilateral withdrawal plan supported by the mainstream conviction that there was no credible Palestinian partner to talk to and pending arrival of one, Israel needed to secure its boundaries and enhance the safety of its citizens, hence the resort to unilateralism. However, this approach was believed to ensure that the maximum of Palestinians live on the minimum of land.[11] As to the peace dividend, the military attacks virtually isolated Palestinian towns, destroyed key infrastructure, preventing commerce and economic activity. In 2002, the International Labour Organization (ILO) estimated the level of unemployment in the Occupied Territories to stand at 43 per cent and the percentage of Palestinians living on less than two dollars a day to be 46 per cent. Predictions were for it to rise to 62 per cent by the end of that year. Another depressing estimation was the fall of the economic output by 12 per cent in 2001.[12] Moreover, the Palestinians in the Occupied Territories suffered further deterioration in quality of life through a regression in their relative democratic rights with continuous Israeli demands to crack down on the militant groups enlisting PNA's abuse of human and civil rights (Nonneman 2001: 153). Above all, security (personal and communal) that is sought out of any peace agreement did not materialize and violence remained the best alternative to a negotiated agreement (BATNA),[13] as could be testified by the outbreak of the second Intifada in 2000.

However, the damage was not only restricted to the economic and political spheres, but also to the future. Observers note that a new Palestinian generation is emerging with militant ideas. This is particularly true of camps in the Occupied Territories. For example, many Jenin refugee camp militants were only pupils during the first Intifada era (1987–93). They were known as the 'children of the stones' who received public admiration and were heroes in the Arab world. By the time the Oslo summit ended, they could hardly read or write and the PNA had no programmes of rehabilitation, making their socio-economic outlook bleak. To them, the Intifada had given them status, a purpose, prestige and an existence whereas the compromise took all that away in exchange for nothing. The siege of 2002 had a most destructive effect on their faith in any compromise, thereby radicalizing them.[14] Moreover, refugee camp inhabitants complain, even in the West Bank and Gaza Strip, of social snobbery with which citizens combine political solidarity, resulting in the treatment of refugee camp dwellers as second- or even third-class citizens. Supporting this attitude is the continuous deterioration in camp conditions because of decreased funding to UNRWA, decreased remittances from relatives working in the Gulf region and damage to camp infrastructure and income sources. Therefore, many yearn for the Intifada, not because they are eager to return to Haifa, for example, but more likely because they want to be heroes again.

Overall, the first decade of formal peace between Jordan and Israel was relatively violence-free. However, this is not to say Jordan remained immune to the violence across the border. Given the atmosphere in the Occupied Territories and deterioration of the peace process, it was difficult to speak of normalization of relations with Israel *after* 2000. By that time, the deadline for final status talks had passed, as had the 'sacred date' (as Arafat would call 4 May 1999) for declaring the establishment of a Palestinian state. From an Arab perspective, progress had only been in continued settlement building and expansion at the expense of effective Israeli withdrawals and proper implementation of joint agreements (Rubin 1997a). By the time the second Intifada started, the popular Jordanian mood was that the peace process had reached a deadlock and was, more or less, doomed (Scham and Russell 2001). Television and newspaper pictures of Israel Defence Forces' actions appalled the public whose sentiments of fury and frustration were already heightened by prospects of an anticipated attack on Iraq (which later materialized).[15] Despite the fact that early on in the process, Jordan criticized the bombings as actions undermining prospects of lasting peace,[16] sympathy later focused on the Palestinians under occupation as a result of continued Israeli closures of Palestinian areas and the disproportionate level of retaliation by the IDF (especially with operation Grapes of Wrath). Such measures were largely perceived as unjustified collective punishment for the acts of a few, reflecting a callous disregard for Arab life. This opinion was supported by the bombing of the refugee shelter in Lebanon, an act very few believed to be a mistake given the Israeli army's flaunted war-technology. Such acts reinforced beliefs that Israelis were anti-peace and as such were, themselves, the obstacle to peace, a situation that lends support to Väyrynen's argument on the difficulty of separating people from the problem especially when dehumanization and demonization are part of the process (Jeong 1999: 152).

Not surprisingly, doubts regarding peace and further normalization were revived and publicly expressed. For example, *Jordan Times'* editorial of 18 April 1996 read 'peace is being shattered in Lebanon'; while the Lower House of Parliament proclaimed the massive Israeli retaliations as an act that 'exposes to the world the true face of the Jewish state'.[17]

This background intensified feelings of hostility towards 'the Zionists' and the Americans, popularly believed to be under the great influence of the pro-Israel lobby (especially the AIPAC) and the executors of their wishes. Qualifying this opinion as exaggerated and overly simplistic is besides the point as what matters, from an analytical point of view, is that it is a widely held perception serving as a lens through which many policies and actions are seen.

The socio-economic dimension: the unripe 'fruits of peace'

Following the peace treaty, Jordan and the United States started to encourage business links between both states. The 1995 Amman Economic Summit witnessed the creation of the Regional Business Council (RBC), which was managed by the Americans to act as a chamber of commerce facilitating meetings, multilateral exchanges and joint business ventures among leading Jordanian, Israeli and Palestinian business groups. As an incentive, the US offered the Qualified Industrial Zones (QIZ) programme, which, as discussed earlier, is considered a success story, eagerly highlighted at every international forum hosted by Jordan, including the World Economic Forum (WEF) at the Jordanian Dead Sea Resort of Shouneh, in June 2003. At the conference, Jordanian officials stressed national accomplishments, especially Jordanian exports to the US which rose from less than US$20 million in 1999 to over US$200 million by 2002 (Moore 2003) with most jobs being taken by women. Indeed, the QIZ story is a success to be replicated anywhere else in the region with anticipated success. Above all, it was made possible through peace with Israel. This prompted many commentators and scholars to declare that Jordan has indeed benefited economically as a direct result of the peace and as such, the fruits of peace were not only ripe for Jordan but also reaped.[18]

However, there is more to the reality of the economic situation during the era of peace. That is, even though the peace treaty was popularly believed to be the means for ushering an unprecedented economic boom in the form of peace dividends, the average Jordanian did not reap the fruits of peace. In fact, economic growth in the second half of the 1990s was lower than in the first half of the decade. The annual growth rate of GDP dropped from 10 per cent during 1992–4 to 5.6 per cent in 1995, then to 1.5 per cent during 1996–8 with the GDP growing slower than the population between 1996–9, which indicated a decline in the per capita income during that period (Mango 2003). By the end of 1997, some 26 per cent of the Jordanian population suffered from absolute poverty while 45 per cent of all families lived on a monthly salary of at most JOD150 (almost US$180). Unemployment remained essentially unaltered, standing at high rates estimated at 20 to 30 per cent.[19] While the drop in the standard of living was a result of a combination of factors not necessarily related to the peace process, the association was nonetheless made between both since the Jordanian economy, as far as the majority of citizens were concerned, was, in fact, worse off in the era following the treaty of peace with Israel (ibid.) and contrary to original expectations.

The 'best years' for trade relations between both countries were, from Jordan's perspective, 1997 and 1998. Even though each party shows different statistics for trade during this period, the exactness of the figures themselves does not matter but rather the indications behind them, namely that not only was trade taking place between both parties but that it was actually slightly in Jordan's favour. Apart from the years 1997–9, Jordanian–Israeli trade has been almost equal in terms of input and output. For example, for the year 2002, total Jordanian exports to Israel amounted to JOD86.3 million with JOD57.7 million (almost US$81 million) in clothing. The JOD57.7 million of exports came from JOD47 million in imports of Israeli textiles. Raw material was returned to Israel without a substantive benefit to the Jordanian market as was hoped, which was not the case in the years from 1997–9. Until the end of 2003, Jordanian imports from Israel were greater than its exports. Ministry of Trade and Industry statistics showed that Jordanian exports to Israel for 2001 totalled JOD72.9 million, while Jordanian imports from Israel in 2001 equalled JOD78.1 million. Jordanian exports to Israel in 2002 equalled JOD86.3 million while Jordanian imports from Israel in 2002 were JOD89.1 million. As for 2003, Jordanian exports to Israel for the year were JOD60.2 million and its imports JOD80.8 million.

Even the QIZ' story has another side to it as more than 80 per cent of the firms located in Jordan's 12 zones are South Asian textile and luggage manufacturers. Nearly half of the 20,000 workers are not Jordanian, and Jordanian workers complain of very low wages (US$3.50 per day) that hardly suffice to cover transport which is not always provided even though workers tend to come from remote areas. On a cultural note, some communities are becoming resentful of the clashing traditions and cultural practices of the foreign QIZ workers whose social habits appear jarring to local customs. Given Israeli closures of the West Bank, QIZ exports did not include Palestinian components (at the time of writing) and manufacturers struggle to ensure Israeli minimum contribution of 7 per cent (mostly zippers, packaging or labels added during export at Haifa port). Since most of the cloth is imported and wages are extraordinarily low, QIZ firms find it difficult to meet the 11.7 per cent domestic content requirement, and thus calls for a lower threshold continue to gain strength. It would seem that QIZ investors reap considerable gains by exploiting resident resources of cheap labour and easy access to US markets. Not surprisingly, the turnover of Jordanian staff at these institutions is very high where a large number of workers remain on the same pay rate and scale for more than three years, making a little over US$100 a month. This is not enough to meet the government's estimated lowest monthly income of US$220 per average household to remain above the poverty line (UNDP Jordan Human Development Report 2004: 96). The fact that many workers at these zones are the sole income providers in their families highlights the gravity of the situation. However, none of the aforementioned is meant to undermine the QIZ experience or its impressive and unprecedented contributions to the Jordanian economy, but rather it is to shed some light to indicate that its positive impacts on the country's macro economy were not entirely cost-free.

The government's raised expectations for the peace dividend were not well founded from the beginning. The World Bank's report of 1994 on the impact of peace on the Jordanian economy stressed that, while gradual growing out of debt was possible for Jordan, it fell short from providing the rapid and sustained growth needed to reinforce peace with Israel.[20] Moreover, Jordan was not eligible for financial pay-offs for entering into an agreement with Israel on a per capita basis (as was the case with Egypt in 1979). The best that Jordan obtained by way of debt relief was cancellation of its outstanding debt of US$702 million to the United States, while the UK, Germany and France approved smaller reductions, with all external debt forgiveness totalling US$800 million. Nonetheless, by 1999, the Kingdom's foreign debt stood at more than 100 per cent of its GDP. While Jordan's good relations with the United States have secured increased economic and military aid,[21] granted aid remained below what was needed to rid the country of its crippling debt burden despite the progress it was making at some economic levels. The key issue was that to the average person, 'there was no noticeable improvement in the standard of living' (ibid.: 264). In fact, with the elimination of subsidies on irrigation water, municipal water and electricity in 1996, many people were worse off[22] despite available figures indicating an improved economy at the macro-level as indicated by the increased Jordanian exports to the United States.[23]

Since the 1950s when Jordan kick-started its modernization through phosphates and potash, it has harboured optimistic economic expectations that were continuously hampered by realities on the ground. In the 1970s, it hoped to be 'the new Beirut' (the banking and financial centre of the Arab world) while in the late 1980s, it was to be 'the Hong Kong of the Levant'. By the 1990s, international donors and US officials were referring to Jordan as a model for economic reform in the Middle East. After the extraordinary World Economic Forum, Jordan was to be the linchpin of the Bush administration's Middle East Partnership Initiative (MEPI) and the *Schwerpunkt* for its envisioned Middle East Free Trade Area: MEFTA (Moore 2003). However, what is sometimes overlooked is that unemployment remains high (around 20 per cent of the labour force) with the per capita income essentially remaining locked at its 1984 levels, despite peaks and valleys (Moore 2003) while population growth remains high.[24] In 1997, the RBC itself collapsed as a result of the continued violence in the Occupied Territories and which, at the time, soured the public opinion on the peace process. As a result, boycotts of Israeli and/or American products became popular through different means including mobile phone messages. Even Jordan's humble and dependent official business group went along with the opposition boycotts. Concerning the QIZ, if investors were having trouble meeting the 11.7 per cent domestic content threshold, it was unclear how they could expect to meet the requirement of 35 per cent under the Free Trade Agreement. Furthermore, it remains unclear how Jordan would cope with competition when Egypt and other Arab partners replicate the QIZ model and offer more 'attractive' conditions (such as much lower local pay scales or better skilled labour).

Indeed, the effort to link trade and peace in Jordan has not been as successful as originally hoped and certainly not the success many observers and analysts claim it to be. Concerning the peace dividend, Jordan did not accomplish the envisaged prosperity. The ultimate dream of a Jordan able to break its dependence upon foreign aid and 'turn its particular combination of human capital, close ties to Israel and poor natural endowment to its long term economic advantage' has yet to emerge (Joffé 2002: 334).

One third of Jordan's US$3 billion in external debt is for the military. The US did not reduce that debt as it did with Egypt (which benefited from a reduction of US$6.5 billion of its US debt after the Gulf war), even though Jordan could certainly have benefited from a similar treatment, especially with precedents available in reducing/rescheduling Israeli, Egyptian as well as Turkish debts owed to the US (see World Bank report 1994: 61). Various programmes were launched, for example, the private investor initiative launched under the motto 'Jordan Vision 2020' with the ambitious goal of raising per capita income to JOD2.200 (roughly twice its present level) by 2020. The campaign proved the King's professionalism at marketing Jordan internationally (e.g. the royal speech at the World Economic Forum) and promoting its information technology sector among some of the field's key international investors. However, these initiatives remained mostly hostage to various structural constraints on the legal, administrative as well as social levels that meant modest success in attracting the required investment or, if attracted, sustaining and maintaining it. Such constraints had a negative impact on one of the Kingdom's most crucial projects: poverty alleviation.

The economic situation in Jordan, overall, lends support to the argument of Benjamin Navon that 'the careful observation of Middle Eastern economic development shows that it is not solely determined by economic polices of governments and other economic variables, but also by political realities' (Joffé 2002: 237). Income from tourism, Jordan's second source of income after the Potash and Phosphate mining industry, fell in 2001 to below the 1996 level. In 2000, tourism sites generated an income of JOD10.8 million (US$15.23 million) and only JOD1.5 million (US$2.12 million) in 2002 as set out in UNDP's Jordan Human Development Report (2004: 39). This was mainly the result of the Intifada across the border, the events of 11 September in the United States and the anticipated, later actual, attack on Iraq, all of which were reasons for embassies to issue travel warnings to their citizens advising against unessential travel to the region. Moreover, young people who entered new employment opportunities in tourism and small enterprises were affected by staff lay-offs and declining trade with the fall in tourist numbers. Therefore, negative impact was not restricted to the economic sphere, but also the social and psychological, as many of these young people overcame difficult social and cultural obstacles to enrol in untraditional professional alleys, re-orienting themselves to the emerging economy. When such risk-taking behaviour goes unrewarded, it can lead to further frustration and dependence (Jordan Human Development Report 2004: 3).

Domestic politics also took their toll, particularly the role of the anti-normalization movement. Having failed to stop the passing of the peace treaty through parliament, the leftist and Islamist groups attempted to organize a conference against normalization, which the government (respectful of the treaty's article II point I.a. calling for the prevention of harmful incitement) banned. The anti-normalization movement had a negative impact on the economy, discouraging direct as well as bilateral investment. Restraining realities as a result of the anti-normalization movement comprised, for example, of the inability of Israeli businessmen to obtain legal advice or representation in Jordan lest the Jordanian lawyer be expelled from the lawyers' association for acts of 'normalization', thereby denying Israeli citizens not only legal advice but also the right to lawful legal representation (supposedly guaranteed by the peace treaty's article 11, point 1d calling for 'due process of law' in both states). These factors made for a tense environment for conducting business, especially against the background of the anti-normalization's 'mother' of all boycotts, namely that of the first Israeli Trade Fair.

The political culture of anti-normalization

Prior to discussing the political culture of anti-normalization, the questions that this section's heading is raising must be answered. The first is why discuss political culture under structural obstacles as opposed to obstacles related to agency? After all, political culture is made up of cognitions, values and emotional commitments of a nation (or group); so would it not be best to discuss this issue within an agency context? Also, does the heading suggest that the nation's mainstream political culture was based on anti-normalization? If so, then how could the Centre for Strategic Studies' public survey findings, referenced in chapter one about people's readiness for peace, be explained?

To answer the first question, one must remember that structures exist at all levels of social interaction and constitute the environments in which agents operate. They define the parameters for action, enabling some and hindering others even at the detriment of personal attitudes. This makes the prominence of an anti-normalization culture in Jordan after formal peace a key structural obstacle to warm peace between both states because its activists institutionalized their opposition to peace and further normalization by imposing laws, rules and regulations upon groups under their influence. This prohibits them from any form of interaction with Israel or Israelis lest the 'psychological enmity' towards the Israelis be reduced. The main reason anti-normalization is not discussed under agency-related obstacles lies in the fact that the institutionalization of this culture by the 'anti-normalization movement' acted as a melting pot for parties traditionally and ideologically opposed but which now found themselves sharing an opposition to peace and/or normalization with Israel (Islamists and Leftists). This unity blurred the distinctions between the various agent groups to the extent that they started to speak the same language. For example, Islamists started arguing that normalization with Israel was based on exploitation, whether economic (e.g. QIZ) or territorial (e.g. Baqura and Al Ghamr). The use of Leftist-based arguments of exploitation as opposed to the more traditional religion-based ones can only be interpreted as a 'pragmatic' evolution bound to appeal to non-Muslims as well as Muslims with varying degrees of Islamist tendencies. Indeed agent particularities dwindled so drastically that differentiating characteristics were no longer easily discernible, hence the inclusion of the anti-normalization culture under structural obstacles.

As to the questions regarding the prevalence and prominence of this culture, there is no denying that the Jordanian mainstream political culture includes deep-seated negative attitudes towards the Israelis, a point duly discussed when reviewing the conflict's history and its psychological dimension. However, in itself, this reality does not conflict with survey results regarding public attitudes towards peace, as the very definition of political culture differentiates it from ephemeral attitudes towards specific issues (which explains why a nation's majority could agree to go to war against one country and a few months later call that decision a mistake and go back on it). Political culture comprises the long-held values characteristic of a whole nation, a group thereof or even a subgroup. Moreover, this book builds upon the premise that the pro-peace groups not ideologically opposed to peace with Israel were so disenchanted with the degree of structural change in the relationship with Israel that the long-held negative attitudes remained intact, making it difficult to generate new interpretive schemes and positive attitudes under the circumstances.

However, it is noteworthy that this section will focus on the official and formal anti-normalization movement itself and which, contrary to common belief, remained more-or-less of a homogenized nature during the first decade of peace. The fact that in the second half of the 1990s it was more pronounced and active than before should not be confused for evolution, but rather a timely manifestation of that which already existed, thereby conveying messages of public and official discontent and disillusionment to the other side.

The obstacle

From the outset of the peace process, two groups were vocal in their opposition to peace with Israel: Islamists and Leftists (the latter describing the secular left which, in Jordan, comprises parties as well as movements with nationalist and socialist ideological orientations). Popularly, they became known as the 'anti-normalization movement' (Mango 2003). Initially, both rejected peace with Israel for different reasons. Islamists opposed it based on ideological religious doctrine they believed to be opposed to peace (i.e. that Palestine and Jerusalem are Islamic lands in need of liberation by holy Jihad); while the Leftists refused it based on their ideologies that tended to oppose Israel's existence. It must be noted here that the majority of Leftists have shown more pragmatism than the Islamists as many mainstream leftist elements accepted the concept of peace with Israel through their acceptance of the 1982 Fez Peace plan espousing the establishment of a Palestinian state on the West Bank and Gaza strip. However, the pan-Arab nationalists and Marxist branches remained opposed to Israel's existence on ideological grounds. Notwithstanding that the majority of Leftist elements had agreed to the concept of peace with Israel, there was a unanimous opposition to the post-Madrid agreements on the grounds of their bias in Israel's favour, negotiated, according to the Leftists, out of Arab weakness, resulting in concessions at the expense of the Palestinian national rights. This gave rise to fears of further Israeli penetration of the Arab nation through political and economic domination that could extend to the realm of culture as well. For example, in his speech following the assassination of Rabin and upon forming his government, Peres spoke of 'The New Middle East' which, in his vision, would be 'dominated by banks, not tanks; ballots, not bullets, and where the only generals would be General Motors and General Electric', words that to many in the Arab world bore a threat. They were understood as meaning a reconstruction of the Middle East with Israel at its centre, feeding fears of a cultural domination that would threaten Arab identity and heritage. Therefore, the anti-normalization movement became a non-violent action that in essence was a technique of struggle.[25]

The movement focused its efforts on robbing the treaty of any social significance by using the influence at the disposal of its members: their civic political bodies, namely, the professional associations,[26] as well as opposition parties and popular societies (e.g. the Anti-Zionism and Anti-Racism Society founded in 1993 by Layth Shubeilat, former head of the Engineers Association and a leading political dissident).[27] The movement's activities took various forms: boycotts, blacklists, public conferences, demonstrations and disbarment of syndicate members for 'normalising relations with the enemy'. Normalization was understood in such basic terms as attending an international conference also attended by Israeli participants[28] or visiting Israel for personal reasons. The movement was particularly proud of its largest demonstration, which took place in January 1997 protesting the opening of the first Israeli trade fair in Amman. An act considered the 'mother of all anti-normalization achievements to date', with the business group at the time calling for a return of the Arab boycott against Israel while pressing for closer relations with Iraq where most entrepreneurs had interests (Bouillon in Joffé 2002: 14). However, expulsion of professional members from their respective syndicate or association was the strongest weapon the movement had and used given that the law in Jordan requires professionals to be members of their associations in order to practice their profession. Therefore, by blacklisting and then expelling members, they would not only have social pressures to contend with, but economic ones as well, given that their livelihoods were threatened. Moreover, the blacklists were also made available to neighbouring Arab countries, displayed on the screens of some satellite channels resulting in Arab boycott of the Jordanian normalizers. In a sense, boycotts and blacklists were the movement's attempts at reviving the policy adopted by the Arab states after 1950 to first boycott shippers carrying passengers or cargo to Israel and later extended to any corporations dealing with Israel. Even though the country's Higher Court of Justice overruled the majority of the expulsions, the fact remained that the incrimination of professionals curbed the extent to which Jordanians supported normalization given the direct risk it posed on their livelihood and social standing in their community and the society.

In 2001, the anti-normalization movement issued a 'black list' naming a number of very high-ranking Jordanian officials identified as 'normalizers', thus making them subject for social, economic and professional boycott, to be redeemed only through the public request of forgiveness. This would normally take the form of a declaration published in the local press along with a pledge to end and cease all dealings with Israel in any context while declaring their support for holy war against Israel and the 'Zionists'. Interestingly, the movement's definition of normalization was broad enough to include 'each practice that removes or lessens the psychological enmity towards the Zionist enmity' (Barari 2004: 43). This meant that all practices with Israel or Israelis fell under the taboo practice of normalization, for example, reading a given book or article would constitute an act of normalization if it resulted in the reader's consideration of certain policies carried out by Israel. At times, the interpretation even extended to the inadmissibility of contacts with Israeli Arabs who, incidentally, count among them Palestinian nationals whose loyalty to the Palestinian cause is well documented including leading Palestinian poets whose patriotic poems used to be taught in schools. This sad reality did not go unlamented by Mahmoud Abbas (1995) who complained of the distorted understanding of who the 'enemy' of peace was. Following the issuing of that list, the government arrested seven of the movement's members on charges of 'belonging to an illegal organization' and 'endangering citizens' lives'.

The official government reaction, however, took place in November 2002 when a Higher Court's Special Bureau for the Interpretation of the Law was requested to interpret the bi-laws of the professionals' associations to determine the legality of the anti-normalization committees[29] and the council of association presidents which issued the boycott and disbarment directives. The committee, made up of the President of the Cassation Court, two other prominent Cassation Court judges, deputy of the interior minister (a law professor) and the director of the legislation department at the prime ministry (also a lawyer) declared the anti-normalization committee illegal and its decisions within the associations and outside null and void. Legal experts also found the Council illegal. The outcome was the disbanding of the anti-normalization committee and twenty other groups within the associations.[30] However, later, Prime Minister Fayez's government appeased the associations, bridging the gap between them and the government by allowing the reformation of the committee only under a slightly modified name: 'The committee for protecting the homeland and anti-normalization'. The compromise between the government and the associations resulted in maintaining the council of association presidents (on the premise that it served only administrative purposes and facilitated inter-association communication) and agreeing that while the anti-normalization committee could call for boycotts, hold lectures, and conduct studies on the importance of anti-normalization, it could not issue blacklists, publish directives to that effect, or expel members.

The argument that the anti-normalization movement grew stronger after Israel's incursion in South Lebanon in 1996 is misleading. This is because the anti-normalization movement came into existence before there even was a Jordanian–Israeli peace treaty. It was determined to prevent such a peace from materializing, and failing that, determined to rob it of any social or tangible significance. Needless to say, continued deadlocks in the Palestinian–Israeli peace process and cooling in Jordanian–Israeli relations boosted the credibility of the anti-normalization slogans that had long declared Israel a partner not serious about peace. With time, the anti-normalization movement was expanding in scope also to include anti-Western policy orientation and relations, especially with the US war on terror and anticipated attack on Iraq. This made it an easy wave to ride to obtain political power and gain economic advantage.[31] Many people interviewed, for example, confirmed that it was enough to insinuate in the yellow press that a person or business had ties with Israel for that business or person to actually be boycotted by consumers and undergo financial bankruptcy, especially when Iraq stopped dealing with all blacklisted business groups or persons.

A weak peace dividend that failed to make its presence felt in the life of the average Jordanian and continued violence in the West Bank and Gaza raised the anti-normalization movement's popularity as was evidenced in the local press. Consequently, the Jordanian parliament was swept up by the rising tide of popular discontent, with many members of parliament asking for the expulsion of Israel's ambassador to Jordan and the recall of Jordan's ambassador to Tel Aviv (a wish half granted when Jordan did not replace its outgoing Ambassador to Tel Aviv when the second Intifada began in 2000). A telling indication was the fate of the promising MENA summits which had to be suspended in the aftermath of the last meeting in Doha in 1997 when (following Egypt and Saudi Arabia's boycott of the proceedings) no participant expressed willingness to host the next conference.

The argument so far has been that the anti-normalization movement presented a formidable obstacle to further normalization. This had an impact on formal bilateral cooperation which, if not hindered, was not made public for fear of popular displeasure. Consequently, many fields of cooperation stipulated in the peace treaty were seriously held back, even in such 'safe' fields as culture and science.

Culture-wise, what materialized was participation in regional projects comprising Egypt, the PNA and Jordan with external funding but not in the form of bi-lateral projects per se; and certainly nothing that approached the letter or spirit of signed agreements. For example, only one Jordanian university lecturer took his sabbatical to spend a year in Israel. Even initiatives that did not involve direct contact, like the Satellite-based Interactive Distance Learning and Training System project (established with the help of the Open University of Israel), did not have more success even though logistical problems were said not to be of the essence.

However, a review of the main cultural activities in the first years of peace reveals much curiosity at the popular level towards that little known yet highly dreaded 'other'. For example, the topics of public lectures offered at Abdul Hameed Shoman Foundation (which hosts widely popular and well-attended lectures by Arab and foreign officials, celebrities or personalities from the fields of politics, art and academia) were mainly on the concept of normalization[32] and its different aspects, a tendency well portrayed in the local press at the time. The issue of complete normalization was, at least, a topic of discussion, a possibility, even if a remote or undesirable one. The resumption of the Intifada in 2000, however, put an end to interest in the topic, shifting attention to the struggle itself, with seminars and lectures organized to commemorate the passage of time marking the beginning of the uprising. The new issue became globalization and the challenges facing the Arabs, especially the Iraq–US dilemma. The shift from the peace process to continued Israeli occupation was reflected in the local press. For example, while some optimism by the Jordanian leadership and government accompanied the arrival of Netanyahu to office, 'cautious' Jordanian hopes marked the beginning of the premiership of Barak,[33] and then hardly any hope with Sharon's election. Following the Intifada in September 2000, most front page headlines and editorials (up until 1 May 2002) focused on the number of daily casualties, damage to property and military means used by Israel in incursions while most editorials concluded that Israel was not ready for peace.

People-to-people contact through tourism did not serve a particularly positive role in dispelling popular misperceptions of the Israelis. For example, the opening of the Southern border meant access by Israeli tourists to the famous Jordanian touristic site, Petra, for day tours that denied local hotels much needed work as the tourists would 'bring everything, including sandwiches and water, with them from Israel' (Mathew Gray in Joffé 2002: 322). Consequently, the Jordanian government raised the entrance fee on popular sites to guarantee a minimum share in costs related to the maintenance of the sites. In Petra, for example, the fee went up from US$7 to US$35. Needless to say, this type of tourism did not help the 63 hotels in the small southern village, all opened in anticipation of an unparalleled boom. The southern Red sea city of Aqaba also failed to benefit from the peace. Next to Eilat, it appeared smaller, much less equipped. In 1994, for example, Eilat had 5,500 hotel beds compared to 1,413 in Aqaba, which had far less restaurants, attractions and a law against gambling. Not only did it not compete numerically, but also qualitatively.

Aggravating matters were the resumption of the Intifada across the border and war on terror, prompting many embassies to issue travel warnings to their citizens. This immediately resulted in tour cancellations to Jordan.

Conclusion

This chapter has argued that despite the success (at the policy level) by the top-level leadership at paving the way for a warm peace between the people of both countries, key structural obstacles hindered normalization of relations at the popular level. The obstacles, discussed from a Jordanian viewpoint, meant that agreements more dependent on mutual popular support met an opposition that denied them the opportunity to rise to expectations. In reality, the success of many agreements was confined to policy level, that is, in their having been reached in the first place and in being implemented, albeit sometimes at a modest level.

What matters is that in the end, the structure of the Jordanian–Israeli relationship was not perceived as changing in favour of Jordanians (regardless of origin); the balance seeming irrevocably tipped against them. This perception had two implications: weak infrastructure for further normalization by those who were not ideologically opposed to it and absence of a cognitive background for changing negative frames and interpretive schemes at the agency level.

5   The refugee question and peace

Jordan is host to the Palestinian refugees who live inside as well as outside the 13 refugee camps. The refugee issue is discussed here from two angles, structural and affective (uncovering the psychological dimension of the dilemma). I will argue that unless the refugee question is resolved holistically and to the satisfaction of the parties concerned, the issue will continue to be surrounded by enough ambiguity to serve as a means for the opposition (mainly Islamists) to rally support against peace with Israel.

The refugee question was traditionally at the heart of the Palestinian conflict with Israel, hailed as the 'pillar of faith' and 'cardinal right' of the struggle. It remains a topic that ignites passions readily and arouses Israeli fears and suspicions of the Palestinian leadership's reconciliation to a two-state solution (since the exercise of the right of the return would mean the demise of the Jewish state). In the 1970s, however, the Palestinian leadership subordinated the primary right of return to that of establishing a Palestinian state and as such, the settlement which brought about realization of that wish, the Oslo Process, meant the end to the unrestricted right of return of all refugees. The Palestinians felt betrayed by their leadership and this Process, which took them by surprise.[1] As'ad Abdul Rahman, former head of the PLO's Department of Refugee Affairs, stated that 'After Oslo, the refugees felt betrayed and sold out. They put us under the whip every place we visited: "You sold us out!"'[2] Not surprisingly, the refugee population became more radicalized in the wake of Oslo as indicated by the fact that most votes by camp dwellers in the second national elections of 1993 went to Islamist candidates. Clearly, the PLO's mantra that the refugee question was 'the central issue' of the Israeli–Palestinian conflict and that the right of return was 'sacred' had indeed taken root within refugee and non-refugee communities, a fact not lost on the PLO itself who many believe would use it to rekindle a spark and start a right-of-return movement to promote its political objectives.[3] However, following the Jordanian–Israeli peace treaty, the overall mood changed to one of optimism in anticipation of a close end to the problem, but with the deterioration in relations and faltering Israeli–Palestinian peace track, the refugee camps were radicalized anew under the influence of the opposition and its anti-normalization agendas.

Definitions and statistics

Refugees (*Laji'un*) are Palestinians who lost their homes in the first Arab–Israeli war (1948–9) fought as a result of the establishment of the state of Israel. The appellation extends to their descendants as well. Those exiled during or since 1967, and their offspring, are known as 'displaced persons' (*nazihun*); a high proportion are 1948 refugees who after 1948 resided in the West Bank and Gaza strip and thus continue to be known as *Laji'un*. Native residents of the Occupied Territories who have not experienced displacement are termed citizens (*muwatenun*) while the PNA personnel returning from exile to the West Bank and Gaza Strip because of the implementation of the Oslo agreements are, irrespective of their places of origin, known as returnees (*A'idun*). An estimate regarding the number of refugees (*laji'un*), considered reliable by most researchers, was produced by the UN Economic Survey Mission of September 1949. In its 'First Interim Report of the UN Survey Mission for the Middle East' (UN Document A/1106) finalized in November 1949, the Mission stated that 750,000 Palestinians became refugees, of which approximately 280,000 went to the West Bank, 200,000 to Gaza Strip, 97,000 to Lebanon, 75,000 to Syria and 70,000 to Jordan, with smaller numbers going to Iraq, Egypt and countries farther afield. Israeli initial estimates were lower, between 520,000 in official estimates and 650,000 in private ones. Palestinians, on the other hand, provided higher estimates ranging between 850,000 to 900,000.[4] After the 1967 war, some 250,000 to 300,000 Palestinians took refuge in the East Bank coming from the West Bank after the war. A similar number of Palestinians returned to Jordan following the Gulf Crisis in the early 1990s.

Unlike Jordan, other Arab countries such as Egypt and Lebanon, have offered citizenship on a selective basis only. In fact, the plight of the refugees was compounded by Arab states' fickle policies, which, for various national reasons, would at times deny issuing re-entry permits to their countries. This was common practice in Lebanon where developing infrastructure within the camps was prohibited, even for the works proposed by UNRWA in the wake of widespread devastation caused by civil war. In Jordan, however, the Palestinian community has produced numerous prime and cabinet ministers, and traditionally dominated the private sector. The refugee camps have principal representative bodies of camp committees (also known as popular or service committees) whose primary function is to act as UNRWA's counterparts to local or national governments with regards to provision of services and welfare to their communities.

Refugee concerns

What do the refugees want? The results of a Palestinian public opinion poll conducted in 2003[5] indicated that if the Palestinian refugees obtained explicit Israeli recognition for the right of return in the context of an Israeli–Palestinian permanent political settlement, only 10 per cent would seek to exercise that right if it meant living under Israeli sovereignty. This meant that the ultimate goal for those most directly concerned might not be the liquidation of the state of Israel. The realization that a two-state settlement and full implementation of the right of return are fundamentally incompatible seems to have induced a pragmatic accept-ance of the necessity of a negotiated compromise on the refugee question, thus paving the way for the 2002 Saudi-launched Arab Peace Initiative which spoke of a 'mutually agreed upon' solution to the refugee problem. Nonetheless, this does not obviate the need for a recognition that harm had been done to them. Perhaps the passionate words of Dabdoub best expose that need:

> We have accepted and recognised Israel, but that does not mean we have forgotten our plight and dispossession. We are not asking to turn the clock back. We are not asking for restitution, not even for an admission of guilt, but we are definitely asking for a recognition that indeed a wrong had been committed. Until that happens, all the efforts will remain in the realm of the condescending at best, or the hypocritical and self-serving at worst.
>
> (Knox and Quirk 2000: 130)

From an Israeli perspective, however, the issue of refugees' return is a highly sensitive issue of existentialism. Official and non-official Israeli declarations leave the Palestinians in no doubt as to where they stand on the issue. Even prominent leaders of the ultra-dovish and staunch peace proponent Meretz party and Peace Now movement published an appeal to the Palestinian leadership on 2 January 2001 in the Israeli daily *Ha'aretz* in which they said: 'We shall never be able to agree to the return of the refugees to within the borders of Israel, for the meaning of such a return would be the elimination of the state of Israel.'

At the practical level, the refugees are most concerned about what the future holds in store for them, especially in light of the deterioration along the Pales-tinian–Israeli peace track. They seek an elaboration on what the proposition of 'settlement' would mean in concrete terms. The approach adopted by the PLO/ PNA was to reaffirm the right of return with broad hints at compromise, thereby failing to win the trust of either the Israeli or Palestinian camp. Refugees seek an explanation from their leadership to what the two-state solution means to them in concrete terms since it is fundamentally incompatible with a full right of return.[6] Relocating to a third country like Canada, for example, is seen as something reserved for the elite among them, while restitution is seen as something that will never reach them but go instead to agencies and various organizations and governments. There is fear of a solution that could mean the end of UNRWA support and the provision of free housing, medical care and education, leaving them destitute.

In Jordan, most refugees focus on the lives they made for themselves there. Unlike in Syria and Lebanon, refugee camps in Jordan have long lost their temporary status with the norm being to build three or four-storey buildings let for residential or commercial purposes. Nonetheless, Jordan's policy has been to refrain from speaking on behalf of the refugee community, insisting on the refugees' right to reach a solution they find satisfying and in line with international legitimacy, warning against the exploitation of the issue by other parties (particularly extremist) to serve their political objectives and promote extremist policies.

The substitute/alternative homeland for the Palestinians

One cannot discuss the issue of the large Palestinian presence in Jordan without discussing another issue of particular concern to the Kingdom: the substitute homeland project.

The idea was first raised in the late 1960s as an Israeli response to concerns regarding the Palestinian issue. The first Israeli to speak of it was Professor Shlomo Avineri, who less than 24 hours after the Karameh clashes, called for it (Bligh 2000: 161). It is noteworthy that Likud always entertained the idea that Jordan was indeed Palestine. The prospect of the East Bank serving as a substitute homeland for the Palestinians was enforced in the Civil War context during which the PLO and certain Israeli policy makers toyed with the idea of an Israeli state discussing with a Palestinian state on the East Bank the future of the West Bank as opposed to the option of an Israeli withdrawal. The PLO, who at the time had little regard for Jordanian state sovereignty, encouraged these ideas. After all, Ahmad Shuqairi, the PLO's first chairman, dismissed Jordan as a country lacking 'the principal foundations of statehood'. The PLO, thus, declared Palestine's true boundaries as stretching from 'the Mediterranean Sea in the west' to the 'Iraqi and Syrian deserts' in the east. Even after the PLO emerged from under the aegis of Nasser, it did not alter its charter or perception of Jordan as an integral part of historical Palestine (Susser 2000: 6). Only in the 1980s were these controversial views removed from the charter. The fear of implementing the substitute homeland plan reigned throughout the 1980s with Ariel Sharon, Israeli Defence Minister at the time, speaking of the need to redraw the Middle East map following Israel's invasion of Beirut (ibid.: 71).

Consequently, the treaty of peace sought a commitment to recognize and respect Jordan's sovereignty, territorial integrity and political independence, ensuring future absence of threat or use of force against it and avoiding involuntary mass movements of people in a way that would endanger the kingdom's security.[7] In reality, the idea was never buried but kept alive by a failing peace process along the Israeli–Palestinian track. Therefore, settlement expansion/ building in the Occupied Territories threatened peace with Jordan, as well as with the Palestinians. According to Professor Joel Beinin of Stanford University, 56 new settlements were established in 2002–3 with most dismantled outposts later rebuilt.[8] With continued Israeli reluctance to relinquish the Occupied Territories in their entirety, ongoing settlement building disturbed Jordan as these settlements constituted national security frontiers and dwelling places for Israelis whom the state could, legally, seek to defend, annexing more of the West Bank territories in the process of doing so.

Though King Hussein was relatively optimistic when Binyamin Netanyahu won in 1996, hoping his arrival would usher a new and promising era of Israeli politics, he quickly changed his mind. Not only were Netanyahu's policies on the ground disappointing, but so were his views regarding Jordan. Netanyahu's book, *A Place Among the Nations,* which was available in Jordanian bookstores, showed its author to be a keen supporter for the 'Jordan is Palestine' idea. More worrying was learning that settlement expansion was not necessarily entirely frowned upon by Labour party figures. Labour's dove Yossi Beilin argued that the Rabin government actually increased settlements by 50 per cent in 'Judea and Samaria' (West Bank) after Oslo, but 'we did it quietly and with wisdom'. He directed blame at Netanyahu saying:

> [you] proclaim your intentions every morning, frighten the Palestinians and transform the topic of Jerusalem as the unified capital of Israel – a matter which all Israelis agree upon – into a subject of world-wide debate
>
> (Chomsky 2003: 195).

The issue, it would seem, was not the expansion of settlement but rather the tactics used, with the doves in Labour favouring 'quiet wisdom' in conducting business.

As far as many Jordanians were concerned, a main ambition behind signing a treaty of peace with Israel, namely securing state sovereignty, remained more or less uncertain. This became more pronounced under the premiership of Ariel Sharon whose arrival to power signalled, from a Jordanian viewpoint, the beginning of a series of attempts at implementing the policy of transfer, hence the military incursions and massive attacks on those most vulnerable (i.e. refugee camp residents) forcing them to leave. One key example is the scale of the attack on Jenin Camp which prompted the UNSC to adopt resolution 1405 following a visit of the senior UN official in the West Bank, Terje Roed Larsen, to the camp in 2002. The resolution noted its concern at the 'dire humanitarian situation of the Palestinian civilian population, in particular reports from the Jenin refugee camp of an unknown number of deaths and destruction'. The UN later estimated that some 497 Palestinians had been killed and 17,000 made homeless (Fraser 2004: 165). The last attempt, however, was the series of unilateral withdrawals and policy of separation. Ironically, this policy, pursued by Likud, brought it closer to its traditional opponent, Labour, with whom it had been growing apart since Oslo. Indeed, pursuit of a unilateral withdrawal from the Occupied Territories and a separation plan appealed to Labour who had both as a contingency plan if a peace accord with the Palestinians failed to materialize. In his speech in August 2001 following his loss to Likud, Barak declared: 'If we do not separate from the Palestinians, this country cannot exist as a Jewish, Zionist and Democratic State' (Rosenberg 2003: 24). The plan also appealed to Likud because it never declared the borders of the separation barrier as the permanent borders of Israel (Beinin 2003). In a nutshell, Robert Frost's 'Good fences make good neighbours' summarizes Israeli mainstream policy despite its negative impacts on the parties involved in the peace process. To Israel, it seemed the only available option in the absence of a Palestinian peace partner.

The Jordanian policy makers as well as the public were doubtful of the genuine absence of an Israeli plan to transform Jordan into a Palestinian homeland, especially when the last Labour Prime Minister, Barak, publicly took pride in being the only Labour prime minister who did not hand over land to the Palestinians. The second man in the Israeli Labour Party, Mr Haim Ramon, also claimed in 1999 that Jordan would certainly be transformed into a Palestinian state in a few years' time (Massad 2001: 272, Fruchter-Ronen 2004).

Indeed, the long-term repercussions of unilateral withdrawal and supporting policies spell trouble not only for the Palestinians, but for the domestic scene in Jordan as well. Not surprisingly, the threat of a substitute homeland still haunts the government and Jordanian public. The *Washington Post* of 30 January 2004 quoted Deputy Prime Minister Marwan Muasher saying:

> We are afraid that the day might come when Israeli leaders might argue 'Jordan is Palestine'… The wall will effectively divide the West Bank into three parts. It will make life impossible for Palestinians, dividing them from their work, their schools, their lands. If that happens, what options do Palestinians have? They will leave, voluntarily or by force, for Jordan.

It is important to remember that while the union years offered breathing space to each community (given the physical presence of two banks where people could split themselves in accordance with their political identities if they so wished), this ceased to be the case after 1967.

6 Leaderships and the peacebuilding process

Top-level leadership

According to Al-Khazendar (1997: 25), 'The paramount role of the King in the formulation of policy means that the role of the Cabinet is essentially executive', a fact confirmed by the constitutional rights granted to the monarch. Therefore, in discussing elite leadership, attention will mainly fall on the person of the monarch who shapes external policies and oversees domestic implementation of ordered reform and progress. However, this is not to say that the elite leadership is reduced to the person of the monarch. The influence of the 'first circle' elite, as Bank and Schlumberger (Perthes 2004) call those advisers, consultants and opinion leaders close to the King, is indeed acknowledged but will not be dealt with separately; rather the final policy tendencies will, understanding that they were shaped by various consultations with members of the political elite. As such, the vision and type of peace envisaged by King Hussein and by King Abdullah II after him are key to this role. These visions become the benchmark against which the degree of implementation is measured.

The King's peace

King Hussein had a vision for peace that he expressed and worked towards achieving. His vision was not limited to Jordanians and Israelis but included all Arabs and Jews. In articulating his vision, he reframed the context of the relationship, seeking to establish a common ground for both the historic warring parties, which meant re-examining history and highlighting moments to which both parties could relate. The goals behind this reframing process were to foster mutual understanding and a degree of compassion that would generate solidarity among people and persuade many into sharing this vision of peace. Consequently, he would repeatedly refer to Muslims and Jews as 'cousins' being the descendants of Prophet Abraham from different wives. The context was now one of warring cousins indulging in a bad family feud that should end, as opposed to a deadly struggle between opposing ideologies, each deeming the other an existential threat. In his keen efforts to create a common bond and foster solidarity, he went as far as saying that both Arabs (Muslim and Christian) and Jews suffered throughout history at the hands of those who colonized or excluded them from their midst. Quite in line with his character whenever he saw a chance of success, he was overzealous and energetic in his efforts. 'Cold peace', similar to the one between Egypt and Israel, was certainly not on King Hussein's agenda. He clearly indicated the type of peace he envisioned saying: 'I can't understand the term "cold peace" ... peace is by its very nature a resolution of all problems ... Real peace is not between governments but between individuals' (Shlaim 2001: 545).

King Hussein actively pursued strategies that would pave the way for full normalization between both peoples. The generous gesture of allowing Israeli farmers to continue using the land they had cultivated in al-Baqura after it reverted to Jordanian sovereignty, while also permitting private land use by Israelis in the Southern area of al-Ghamr for twenty-five years are but indications of the eagerness to resolve questions that could come to represent serious bilateral issues of concern. Months before the treaty was formally signed between the two states, business groups were encouraged to engage in trilateral contact in the hope that they will embark on joint ventures that would support the peace process. The confidence-building measures initiated between the time of the Washington Declaration and the actual treaty signing ceremony months later were signs of the leadership's determination to achieve a warm peace.

Once peace was formal, the government vigorously pursued the elimination of all obstacles at policy level, abolishing boycott laws and other legal impediments that could hinder peacebuilding. So genuine was this endeavour that ceremonies characteristic of the pre-peace era were discouraged. Warm peace was actively pursued at the highest levels, if not 'rushed' into as some critics later declared. Indeed, the clampdown on the opposition (whose main agenda was the country's foreign policy regarding Israel) and relevant control measures adopted were proof enough of the determination to pave the way for normalization and give 'true peace', as King Hussein would call it, a chance after decades of bloodshed and hostility. Undoubtedly, King Hussein believed the time for peace between Israel and the Arabs had come and, as such, it should be heralded as quickly and firmly as possible. Supporting this line of thinking was the ongoing Oslo process and prevalent optimism at the time.

Of particular significance was the role played by King Hussein in securing the Israeli public's approval and respect (a consideration many faulted Arafat for not having) as indicated by his timely visits to Israel. It is worth noting here that while Rabin shared a similar understanding of the role a leader could play in winning the trust and confidence of the other party, no Israeli leader after him exhibited a similar understanding. First, Netanyahu's serious undermining of Jordan's security and sovereignty by going through with the attack against Mashal (also embarrassing the King with Dori Gold's visit shortly before opening the Hasmonian Tunnel), then Barak insensitively appointed Danny Yatom, the former head of Mossad who masterminded the botched attempt against Mashal, to be in charge of Jordanian–Israeli relations. Indeed, given that foreign policy tends to be centralized at the highest level of polity in each state, it is the personality at the helm that matters. Close personal ties between Rabin and King Hussein pushed the peace forward and enabled them to overcome possible impasses, but thereafter, relations began to cool and then deteriorated as explained in earlier chapters. Because King Hussein enjoyed much respect and credibility among the Israeli people, his interventions at key junctions in the Israeli–Palestinian process (e.g. the Hebron Agreement, Wye River Agreement) made some progress possible. His presence had, to a considerable extent, a neutralizing effect on the internal Israeli coalitions.

King Hussein enlisted support for his peace policies in other tacit ways including combating radicalism and the anti-peace ideology. The King (in key public speeches) spoke of his sense of betrayal after all his efforts to end the Israeli–Arab conflict – a theme the majority of East Bank Jordanians, in partic-ular, could relate to – and he complained of the little regard others showed for his people's sacrifices for the sake of Arab solidarity and the Palestinian cause. Drawing a clear link between himself and his people, he spoke of his good efforts to represent the Palestinian brothers only to be turned down in favour of the PLO. His attempts at finding an Arab solution for the Iraqi occupation of Kuwait were not heeded by Arab states in 1989 and resulted in the estrangement of him and his country. These themes were evident in his historic address to the nation in November 1994 in response to the signing of the peace treaty with Israel in which he spoke of the hypocrisy of the 'ungrateful' who criticized Jordan for making peace with Israel even after the Palestinian leadership did so, overlooking the Hashemite and Jordanian efforts throughout the years to safeguard Arab, Muslim and Palestinian interests in Jerusalem and elsewhere. He said: 'We have been at the receiving end of the negative attitudes of others, and of their lack of clarity, their waste of opportunities, their reliance on unbridled emotion, their superficial approach to the future and to our nation's destiny.'

This was the prelude to commending those Jordanians who lived under 'the harshest of conditions' and yet 'have fiercely and obstinately defended themselves and their leadership' (Shlaim 2001). In underscoring the theme of solidarity, he indirectly stressed the need to preserve it in times of peace just as it helped them to remain united in times of war.

In this context, it is noteworthy that the ties linking Jordanians to their King are rooted in religious factors (the Hashemite lineage), cultural factors (the King being head of the Jordanian family, sheikh of the Jordanian tribe[1]) as well as economic ones (since the King heads the army, civil and security services, all being primary employers of Jordanians). However, the affiliation is strengthened through psychological factors that consolidate certain perceptions of self and the other as well as sense of identity and threat, which many of the King's statements underscored, as the above examples demonstrate: that is, Jordanians can relate to the King's sense of betrayal. After all, although the Jordanian army fought bravely in 1948–9, preserving the West Bank and Jerusalem, Arab parties accused it of cowardice. Al-Karameh was another victory in which Jordan played a key role but the PLO and Fatah refused to acknowledge it at the time. The attempted takeover by the Fedayeen, in particular, was a stab in the back, repayment of popular support, sacrifices and solidarity by ingratitude. The King would, therefore, repeatedly describe the army in his speeches as the symbol of 'pride and dignity' and his 'companion' through the country's peaks of glory with their sense of 'true belonging and unshaken loyalty'.[2] The monarch did not only appeal, with such declarations, to the sense of pride and honour inherent in the traditional belief system of Jordanians, but he also delivered a message that Jordan sacrificed enough and deserved to reap the fruits of peace; therefore, it must remain opposed to those embracing anti-peace ideologies and those who ignore the fact that the party most directly concerned, Palestinians, signed a peaceful declaration of principles with Israel.

In a landmark speech in 1998, addressing members of the executive, legislative and judicial branches, King Hussein again denounced allegations directed at the regime and the army saying: 'I believe that this wronged country, which made great sacrifices, constituted at one time a sort of burden on its brothers' as opposed to a source of solace. Not only were Hashemite/Jordanian actions met with ingratitude, but the very little that Jordan had was envied. To Jordanians, the words hit a raw nerve.

Naturally, such passionate and lucid rhetoric helped build the charisma King Hussein enjoyed domestically, a factor that considerably boosted his persuasion abilities. Not surprisingly, one heard many quoting the King in support of their personal views on the issue of peace with Israel.

Other subtle forms of support for normalization were expressed at occasions such as the awarding of the Medal of Independence of the First Order to Mr Hisham Yanis of Nabil and Hisham Theatre Troop, an act that helped the troop fight off repeated attempts by the professional associations to close down the theatre. Other symbolic gestures included visiting the bereaved Israeli families in the wake of the attack against their daughters on a school trip to al-Baqura as well as, years earlier, speaking at Rabin's funeral, lamenting the role of violence in obstructing peace.

King Abdullah II shared the same beliefs and continued on the same path, reconfirming his commitment to the peace process in general and normalization in particular at both the international and domestic levels. This had a positive knock-on effect on other forms of support for peace and normalization where support bases were reassured and security apparatus was in control of the domestic scene during critical times (characterized by deadlocks along the Palestinian–Israeli peace track). Against this backdrop, the closure of Hamas offices in Jordan only months after acceding to the throne and expulsion of its leaders to Qatar count as historic confidence-building measures, moves that displayed intolerance of anti-peace actions and ideology especially following talk of Hamas-planned suicide attacks against foreign targets.

Evaluating King Abdullah's approach to the peacebuilding process reveals him to have a pragmatic mindset. He realized early on that peace was failing to produce the desired economic dividends, causing him to shift focus to the domestic potential, seeking to build a more capable, investment-enticing Jordan not necessarily dependent upon its neighbours west of the river. Thus, he continued in hosting major economic events during low points of the Israeli–Palestinian relations. Proving this tendency, King Abdullah visited Israel fourteen months after his accession to the throne, despite the great impatience on the western border.

King Abdullah represented different things to different audiences, a fact enhancing his power base of support. Internationally, he is the West's ally in its War on Terror, showing domestic signs of intolerance of the Islamists' anti-peace ideologies and the extremists' glorification of violence. However, in concession to the domestic and regional mood, his cooling down of relations with Israel in the wake of the second Intifada and not naming an Ambassador to Tel Aviv appealed to popular Arab and Islamist sentiments, especially the role Jordan played in leading the opposition to the separation wall built by Israel.

In summary, while King Hussein constructed a vision of 'warm peace' for which he sought support, King Abdullah II had a pragmatic vision of a 'functional peace' that he vigorously pursued domestically as well as internationally preserving the foundations of peace during the hardest of times – when the conflict was domestically recast by its supporters as 'zero-sum' after the building of the wall,[3] – an impressive feat by a monarch who had just acceded to power amidst mounting challenges domestically as well as internationally.

Constraining factors

Notwithstanding the support for peace and normalization at policy level by both monarchs, it would be inaccurate to assume that pro-peace policies were ready for effective implementation on the ground. As discussed earlier, until 28 November 2002, the government policy towards the associations, the leading civic representatives of the anti-peace camp, was mainly appeasement as testified by, for example, reluctance to react to the associations' custom of expelling members for being 'normalizers'. This appeasement was probably in light of government realization that outlets were needed in the absence of an opposition in Parliament.

Inefficient bureaucracy

Certain domestic structures had a restraining impact on the degree of normalization. They comprised inefficient bureaucracies that failed to rise to the new challenges of the post-peace era. One key example was the failure by the Institute of Standards to translate its standards (which numbered around 1000) into English to facilitate cooperation with non-Arab counterparts, leaving the applied Jordanian standards unknown to the Israeli side, making it difficult to accept them, especially in light of the very rigorous standardization practices applied in Israel. This caused delays in obtaining the required documentation for Jordanian exported goods, resulting in critical loss of time that could have boosted their competitive edge.[4] Despite signing a trade agreement, there also was no customs clearance office at the northern border for Israeli imports coming through the north of Jordan, necessitating the temporary solution of setting up a customs clearance office at Al-Hassan QIZ. Bureaucratic constraints always had a negative impact on the Jordanian economy especially in terms of attracting foreign investment, a key Jordanian weakness which the country continues to work on improving, highlighting whatever key accomplishments it achieves in that regard. Despite vigorous campaigns to promote investment in Jordan, the various Jordanian governments seem to be lagging behind when it comes to implementing economic and structural reforms (e.g. merging duplicated government institutions, etc.) that are prerequisites for enticing investment.

Compounding the problem was the role of nepotism, favouritism and corruption in government institutions. King Hussein would commission (since the late 1980s) in each letter to a newly appointed prime minister the end of corruption, favouritism and nepotism. The effective implementation of new laws and regulations was at times hostage to personal interpretations by officials who used existing vagueness to permit biased treatments. King Abdullah II had the same penchant for fighting corruption and nepotism, setting up institutions that monitor public and private sector performance. However, socio-political considerations, economic realities and cultural particularities continued to pose various challenges that slowed progress.

Middle-level leadership

The role of the anti-normalization movement led by the mid-level leadership figures within the professional associations was already discussed, thus this section will turn to the role of the other middle-level leadership figures, mainly nationalist and business group leaders, whose overall role had much less impact on the peacebuilding process. As illustrated earlier, the business groups' involvement was greatly hindered by the anti-normalization movement. This movement made it its business to publish names of 'normalizers' who had business ties with Israeli firms, requesting the public to boycott them and their products, offering a list of available substitutes of these imported/manufactured products. Fear of massive consumer boycotts (encouraged by emails and mobile phone messages) beyond the government's help, as well as obstacles taking the competitive edge away from business dealings with Israel were key factors for business groups shying away from assuming a leadership role in encouraging further normalization with Israel. Only 5 per cent of Jordan's export–import community actually established business ties with Israeli counterparts with details of the cooperation remaining unpublicized.[5] The nationalist discourse had its home-based concerns that made the peace process more pressing. Most of the Jordanian nationalists (i.e. those who argue that Jordan is for Jordanians, albeit with different views on how to solve the refugee problem), apart from those who were members of the anti-normalization movement, were not ideologically opposed to normal relations with

Israel. Happy with the fact that Jordan regained its territorial as well as water rights in the treaty with Israel, they still judged the peace process in relation to that dormant threat of a substitute homeland. Therefore, when threats to implement the project increased, they joined the anti-normalization movement mainly to pressure Israel into meeting the Palestinian demands to allay the group's own fears with regard to the domestic threat.

Views of the future

The purpose of this book was never to anticipate or define the shape of peace to come but to lay down markers for what needs to be taken into consideration in order to achieve a warm peace. Therefore, this section will address the question of what the different levels of leadership see as a prerequisite for a warm peace or impetus in pushing the Jordanian–Israeli relations forward.

There exists a consensus among top-level leadership figures, when interviewed for writing this book, over the need to resolve the Palestinian–Israeli conflict. The establishment of a Palestinian state and a satisfactory resolution of the refugee question are fundamental requirements without which attempts at normalization will remain devoid of popular consent and engagement. Although opinions vary (depending on whom one asks) on the specifics of the envisaged solutions (e.g. exact borders of the Palestinian state, etc.), the consensus was that they should be addressed in a decisive manner. Provisional solutions are not recommended. This means, however, that the Jordanian leaders believe that a warm peace is chiefly dependent upon Israeli actions since no such peace is possible unless Israel allows the establishment of a Palestinian state and resolution, inter alia, of the refugee problem.

There was consensus on the need to meet Jordan's economic needs and to keep promises once given in that regard. As some pointed out, Jordan rushed into normalization expecting Israeli development plans of the Wadi Araba to materialize (i.e. the old pledge to have the desert bloom) as well as a fulfilment of the US promise of helping Jordan abolish all its foreign debt, not just that to the United States. Therefore, the resolution of pending political dilemmas and an encouraging peace dividend were unquestionable requirements for a warm peace. In short, people must witness a positive impact on their living standards that could be attributed to peace.

Another point of consensus was the need for the United States to be more involved and determined to have all parties adhere to signed obligations and to stand united facing violence. On 28 September 2003, the third year of the second Intifada was marked with sporadic demonstrations and outbursts taking place in various areas of the West Bank and Gaza Strip. However, the opinion among experts and observers stationed in the West Bank continued to be that the Intifada is very weak, if not dead. It no longer enjoyed the massive popular support of the first Intifada or its level of organization and planning. Parties calling for demonstrations were described as 'out of touch with the people' and the reality on the ground (Allen 2003). There was intense frustration at the indifference among people towards the Intifada in the Occupied Territories. The Intifada yielded no tangible results apart from heavy Israeli retaliation. Moreover, the economic situation is constantly deteriorating because of closures and curfews that confine people to their houses for days on end. Disappointment with the Intifada and its results, however, did not equate with support for acts of violence perpetrated by Islamist groups against Israeli civilians. These acts were questioned by the general Palestinian public, especially following the four suicide bombings of 4 October 2003, which killed 19 Israelis including Israeli-Arabs in Haifa. However, the point to remember here is that, while many at the popular level see no use in the ongoing Intifada or violence, they are loath to see them go, an opinion equally shared by the residents of refugee camps in Jordan. Public opinion seems to indicate the pervasive belief that there is no alternative for confrontation because the end of violence would mark the end of any serious pressure on Israel to compromise (Lori 2003: 26). This, in turn, suggests the need for the peace process to resume on track, undeterred by violence, with enough international support in the form of active implementation-monitoring groups and peacekeeping units as well as economic support to strengthen the peace camps on all sides.

Certain figures of the political elite hold that warm peace is not that hard to achieve, confirming that no compelling reasons exist to prevent a warm peace from materializing once the key Israeli–Palestinian issue is resolved. However, this view was not very common among many from the middle-level leaderships in academia who argued that it would be difficult to undo decades of conditioning in favour of an overnight perception of Israel as a friend. On the other hand, there were those who argued that resolution of the Palestinian problem in particular would immediately remove the highest percentage of the obstacles to a warm peace between Jordanians and Israelis with the advanced economic situation taking care of the remaining percentage.

Some argued that governments could play a positive role by explaining the value of the peace dividends Jordan would reap at the macroeconomic level through, for instance, debt cancellation and annual aid-packages. Many Jordanians felt exploited and cheated (Barari 2004), a feeling sustained by failure to explain the significance of peace to Jordan in practical terms given that initial promises did not materialize. Ian S. Lustick, in Binder (1999: 341), argues that 'gross discrepancies' between prevailing conceptions and 'stubborn realities' translate into difficulty of sustaining beliefs that too explicitly, directly and systematically are contradicted by immediate perceptions. The description fits the economic and political situations perfectly when applied to the Jordanian context. Peace failed to translate favourably at the micro level while politically the conflict was crawling back into its zero-sum context, hence the added significance of highlighting gains from formal peace.

The political middle-level leadership, however, exhibited no particular consensus, being divided into ideology-based opposition (anti-normalization movement of Islamists and Leftists) and nationalists. The Islamist opposition figures interviewed expressed the view that they were not opposed to peace and normalization with Israel but had one condition: that it be the state of all its citizens by law and name as opposed to a Jewish state, that is, if the Jewish state is dismantled and mandatory Palestine returned to its pre-1948 status. To them, the Palestinian National Authority negotiations and deals over a Palestinian state were unjustified and unholy as the entire area between the Jordan River and the Mediterranean should be 'Palestine'. The non-ideology-based nationalists, on the other hand, have more pragmatic requirements. They see no harm in normalizing relations with Israel whose existence is a reality they accept, but require that a Palestinian state be established to gather the Palestinians in exile.

Conclusion

A disconnection between the state-level vision of peace and its implementation, especially at society-level, characterized the process. The peacebuilding processes remained limited in terms of the reality of peace and its implementation on the ground, especially at the affective level. Indeed, the foundations for a warm peace were constantly challenged by lingering emotional ties of a supra-national quality (such as a pan-Arab identification), various currents towards Jordanian nationalism and different orientations and layers of the decision-making system.

7 The road to a warm peace

The book set out to explore why a 'warm peace' failed to materialize between Jordan and Israel, ten years into formal peace and despite a treaty – approved by majority vote in each country – laying the foundations for such a peace. An enquiry was launched, rooted in the Jordanian scene, with an eye on identifying structures and agency factors of relevance. The findings showed that the structure of the relationship between Jordan and Israel remained asymmetric. From a Jordanian perspective, it was not equal but still in favour of the Israeli party. That is, the raised expectations on the political and economic fronts did not materialize. Furthermore, the peace process deteriorated between the Palestinians and Israelis with a negative impact on the Jordanian–Israeli track, which revived public fears for the implementation of the alternative homeland project. Earlier chapters illustrated how the relations cooled between top-level leadership in both states, to the extent that certain Jordanian leaders feared that they 'rushed into' rapid normalization with Israel. Economically, Israel was able to maintain its monopoly over the Palestinian markets, safeguarding its interests by a number of procedures, which deprived outside competition of a viable edge. Moreover, the Jordanian democratic process set in motion in the late 1980s was constrained in the era of peace mainly so Jordan could maintain its pro-peace foreign policy in the face of the local opposition whose programmes subordinated national interests to extremist or radical ideologies. The majority of those not ideologically opposed to normalization of relations with Israel considered peace with the latter too costly and with no tangible return at the micro-level (especially the *quality* of life) despite the economic and strategic gains the country secured at the macro level. The power asymmetry combined with unfavourable domestic factors (particularly the strong political culture of anti-normalization enshrined in the professional associations' laws of boycott and disbarment of members) made it increasingly difficult to push for further normalization at a time when peace itself was becoming hard to keep, let alone promote. Although Jordan completed a full-fledged peace treaty, it remained hampered by domestic exigencies that largely shaped the peace to come. Key among these particularities is the demographic make-up of the society, which presented a formidable structure. This came atop other endemic structural factors like a weak civil society versus overpowering professional associations with an anti-normalization agenda opposed to all forms of contact with Israel, which precluded the possibility of establishing links with the Israeli civil society in a way that could sensitize each party to the other's needs.

While differing political identities had initially encouraged many (especially Israelis) to contemplate a warm peace between Jordanians and Israelis irrespective of development along the Israeli–Palestinian track, the truth was different. If anything, results indicated that the derailment of the Israeli–Palestinian track had a negative impact on the *type* of peace between Jordan and Israel since the non-ideological opposition groups, who had reserved their judgement of the peace process until later, measured progress against their ultimate goal from peace. Progress was thus measured against the group's ultimate goal from peace. In the Jordanian case, there was a definite absence of threat to identity and state versus Palestinian demands for an end to the occupation, establishment of a Palestinian state and a satisfactory resolution of the refugee problem and other pending issues. Though lines intersected and other wishes existed (e.g. improved economic conditions, more personal freedoms, etc.), these were the primary measures against which the peace process was evaluated by both communities in Jordan. These communities had long lists of grievances that showed how their fears were not allayed and concerns legitimized. The Jordanian–Palestinian–Israeli peace tracks are so intertwined that for a warm peace to succeed between Jordan and Israel, the Palestinian–Israeli conflict must first be resolved. Such is the required sequence of events as yielded by the study at hand. Despite existing strong nationalist tendencies, the degree of peace's warmth is dependent upon popular involvement in the process, which in itself is largely tied to events across the border.

In short, the book has argued that the degree of structural change envisaged to encourage full normalization did not take place. If anything, the deterioration in Jordanian–Israeli relations and derailment of the Palestinian–Israeli peace track made long-held negative cognitive beliefs more enduring and popular ideological beliefs more credible. Other regional developments fed this anti-normalization sentiment and political culture, for example, the war on Iraq in 2003. The images of the suffering of 'Arab Brethren' across eastern and western borders of Jordan filled television screens and the front pages of the daily press, serving as a constant reminder of the Arab's overall historic inability to shape their own destiny and the overwhelming omnipotence of the 'colonial' powers and their regional arm: Israel. This guaranteed the anti-normalization movement in Jordan more popular support across all communities.

The Jordanian case study clearly shows that an elite deal can bring about a formal peace following a violent and asymmetric conflict, but without active positive engagement from the various sectors of society, a warm peace remains elusive. However, considerable active involvement is not possible before addressing the structural imbalances and allaying direct and indirect fears of threat. A shift in paradigm from a cold or official peace to a warm one was unlikely to happen in Jordan when Israel was mostly regarded as maintaining the upper hand politically as well as economically. Israel appeared unchallenged in its disregard for the will of others especially when adopting measures seen as threatening to the state and identity of the other parties involved. This means that much need to be done to remove the process from the zero-sum frame and to recast the conflict as one over issues as opposed to non-negotiable principles that transcend time and space, generalized beyond the specific actions of personalities or groups to an entire race. This is now more crucial than ever, especially with the rise of Islamist radicalism.

Concluding remarks and forward-thinking

In 1994, a majority Knesset vote regarding Israel's treaty with Jordan encouraged Jordanian officials to declare that the treaty secured Israeli recognition of Jordan's sovereignty, territorial as well as political integrity. The breakdown of the peace process along the Israeli–Palestinian track, however, and the erection of the separation wall belied this claim.[1] Israeli leaders, therefore, must realize that a Jordanian–Israeli track cannot be pursued separately from an Israeli–Palestinian one if warm relations are sought. For full normalization to be pursued, it must be acknowledged that a real threat from domestic opposition is limited and even irrelevant. Following the second Intifada, the dominant public sentiment in Jordan was anti-normalization (if not anti-peace) joined with a strong conviction that Israel was not serious about peace with the 'Arabs'. A state-centred approach can maintain formal peace but it is not sufficient on its own to yield and sustain a warm one. While those opposed to peace with Israel on an ideological basis are a minority, it is the combination of bloodshed and the breakdown of the Israeli–Palestinian track as well as a weak peace dividend that have disappointed the pro-peace camp. The Israeli–Palestinian track would now have to yield enough progress to convince people that 'true peace' is still feasible.

Jordan's strategic interests require the establishment of a viable Palestinian state. However, it must be acknowledged that the creation of a Palestinian state has also become a strategic Israeli objective since Israeli control of Palestinian lands or annexation thereof would mean a de facto bi-national state. The consensus among Israeli leadership figures from various sectors (especially politics, security and academia) is to avoid the prospect of bi-nationality as confirmed at the Herzliya conference of December 2000. Consensus at this conference was to ensure that the Israeli state's boundaries guaranteed a Jewish majority within. This primary conclusion was shaped by the assumption that the Palestinians would become a clear majority in the year 2020, according to Professor Arnon Soffer who argued that Jews would constitute 42 per cent of the population of historical Palestine by 2020 with an estimated total population of 15.2 million.

However, another conclusion can be drawn from this line of thinking, namely that while a minority calls for expelling Palestinians from their land, this opinion might become a mainstream position in the next two decades if a bi-national state scenario is to be avoided. The key obstacles to Israelis in realizing the outcome (between 2000 and 2003 – the period covered by the research) were continued Palestinian attacks and a belief of absence of a suitable Palestinian counterpart to negotiate with as long as Arafat remained at the helm of Palestinian leadership. Surveys in Israel showed that 90 per cent of Israeli Jews regarded Arafat as a terrorist, a view shared by 75 per cent of voters on the left.[2] This impasse was detrimental to the process and encouraged unilateral Israeli moves, particularly withdrawals from occupied territories without prior consultation with the Palestinians. These, in turn, feared having a state in the end with no viable conditions for survival and attaining sovereignty merely in name.

Benny Morris, a former leading Israeli Revisionist historian, believes the transfer of the Palestinians under occupation to neighbouring states, especially Jordan, will take place (Barari 2004: 95). This point of view was seconded by many in Jordan who thought that Israel repeatedly tried to instigate a civil war in the Occupied Territories and when it failed started to build a wall, all for the purpose of imposing a de facto transfer. From a Jordanian standpoint, Labour and Likud seem united in their understanding of the need for a 'defensive shield'. Following Labour's resignation from Sharon's coalition government on 20 October 2002, Labour's prime candidate, Amram Mitzna, proposed a deadline for agreement with the Palestinians, failing which a security fence would be erected (Fraser 2004: 167). Sharon's landslide victory over Labour (40 Knesset seats versus 18) enabled him to implement his own plan which, interestingly, reconciled the wishes of the old rivals: Labour and Likud. The wall appealed to Labour who considered it a shield against the attacks and a chance to withdraw from Palestinian areas, and it appealed to Likud since the shield's route is not declared the permanent boundary of the Israeli state.[3] Jordan presented a strong case before the International Court of Justice against the wall based on five legal arguments: the principle that the court had the authority to rule over the legality of the wall; the fact that the West Bank is occupied, as opposed to disputed, territory; the illegality of settlements; the illegality of the wall and the need to remove it (Barari 2004: 97). The Court accepted all arguments and ruled against the wall.

The work presented here shows that the potential for a warm peace between Jordan and Israel is not lost but merely waiting to happen if enough obstacles in its path are removed. After all, the similarity in the general atmosphere in the Middle East in 1994 and 2003 is striking, notwithstanding the ups and downs in regional and international developments. The atmosphere in the Middle East in 1994 was characterized by a decline in the Arab–Israeli conflict as a result of the diplomatic breakthroughs, higher priority to economic development in tandem with the rise of individual nation-states (voicing and pursuing their own interests), the weakening of radical states and a new pattern of Persian Gulf security. Furthermore, dropping income in rich Arab states meant less financial support to poorer states and an inclination to invest where profits were highest, pushing states dependent on aid towards more international debt as well as the prioritization of economic reform. Since the latter required stability, peace and good relations with the West were pursued, guided by national interest of state and, subsequently, regime survival. In

1994, King Fahd of Saudi Arabia, in a message to the pilgrims in Mecca, sought religious justifications for these orientations saying:

> well-being of [Muslims] is contingent upon stability, tranquillity and pros-
> perity arising from true faith in Allah .... [Islam] neither encourages sowing
> the seeds of rancour and hate between countries and peoples nor does it
> impose a ban on dealing with others just because they happen to be different
> from us with regard to their orientation and thoughts.
>
> (Rubin, 1997b)

The plea for a moderate interpretation of Islam was the prelude to commending the peace process as the 'beginning of a new phase of coexistence and the transla-tion of peace efforts into real on-the-spot practices ... We are confident that our Arab brothers want peace and are keen on achieving it' (ibid.).

The war on Iraq did not result in massive uprisings in the region, and the public were to a great extent restrained, testifying to their regimes' successful control of the situation and the defeat of pan-Arabism at the implementation level. However, regional power allocations have shifted in favour of Iran. This is seen by many (including the United States and its allies) as an impetus for moving along the peace track with Israel to pre-empt a rising Persian hegemony from playing a key role in shaping the region's future through its proxies and allies, especially in countries bordering Israel. The fact remains that hope for sustainable peace exists as the protracted Arab–Israeli conflict has gone through positive, historic developments. The PLO's ultimate goal of one Palestinian state over all of manda-tory Palestine had been relinquished in favour of a two-state scenario with shared sovereignty over Jerusalem. At the same time, Likud seems to have outgrown its role of a party once beholden to the dream of Greater Israel. After all, Likud's Ariel Sharon was the first to evacuate settlements from 'Eretz Israel', later with-drawing from Gaza. However, effective and capable leadership is a fundamental requirement, without which dangerous splits and divisions among the Palestinians will ensue. This would shake the very foundations of peace, especially if the ideo-logical opposition groups, particularly Islamists, continue to gain in strength and popularity. On the Israeli side, an exceptional leader is required, one who could secure the Israeli public's approval for the necessary concessions that peace with the Palestinians demands. Given the complexity of the Israeli political structure (evidenced in the electoral system), a leader who could bridge the gap between the extremes on both the left and right is needed. Such a leader would reassure the public and bring them along on the road to sustainable peace and reconciliation. In short, peace is a reality on the ground and demands more careful and dedicated efforts to build it. In his address to the nation on 15 November 1994, King Hussein said of the peace that it would not be:

> simply a piece of paper ratified by those responsible, blessed by the world. It
> will be real, as we open our hearts and minds to each other, as we discover a

human face to everything that has happened and to each other – for all of us have suffered for far too long.

At least the path towards such a peace has been charted by formal agreements. It is now more feasible than ever for a 'true' peace to materialize after addressing the key concerns to the satisfaction of all parties concerned. The book has been but a humble attempt at understanding what those concerns and needs are from one key perspective of relevance: Jordanian.

Notes

1 Introduction

1 Johan Galtung defines conflict to refer to a belief or understanding that parties are pursuing common yet conflicting goals with attitudes, behaviour and contradiction being the components of a full conflict.
2 Ninety per cent of Jordanian territory has less than 200 millimetres of rain per year. The average amount of rainfall per year is about 8,500 million cubic metres, 90 per cent of which evaporates, 5 per cent is lost in surface run-off and only 5 per cent recharges the underground water systems through seepage. Therefore, rain-fed agriculture in Jordan does not exceed 5 per cent of the total surface area (Eugenia Ferragina, 'Social adaptive capacity to water crisis', in G. Joffé (ed.) (2002: 347)), making water a strategic issue directly related to state security and survival.
3 See, for example, *The Jordan Times*' leading editorials between 31 October 1994 and 2 November 1994.
4 The war of 1948 produced almost one million Palestinian refugees, 70,000 of whom resided in the East Bank. The 1967 war, however, forced 260,000–300,000 Palestinian from the West Bank and Gaza to move to Jordan. Up until the mid-1980s, the Kingdom witnessed a continuous flow of Palestinians across the bridges, making Jordan the largest host country of Palestinian refugees. In the early 1990s, some 250,000–300,000 Palestinians returned to Jordan from the Gulf, especially Kuwait, following the Gulf Crisis (Susser 2000). According to the United Nations Relief Works Agency (UNRWA), from nearly 3.9 million registered Palestinian refugees in 2001, more than 1.6 million were residing in Jordan (http://www.un.org/unrwa). In 2003 it increased to 1.7 million – almost 42 per cent of Palestinian refugees everywhere.
5 This view was confirmed to the author by prominent Jordanian political analysts and historians interviewed in December 2004 in Amman.
6 Some authors prefer the use of different terms for some of these stages, while many use the last two terms interchangeably.
7 To Lederach, immediate action ranged between 2 and 6 months, while short-range planning required one to two years. Five to ten years and decade-thinking as well as generational vision of twenty years and more are the units required for true reconciliation and a new start

2 The long journey to peace: Jordanian–Israeli relations until the Treaty of Peace of 1994

1 Though the historic overview begins, selectively, and for purposes of brevity, from the early twentieth century, it is noteworthy that the history of Transjordan/East Bank as well as the Zionist movement goes much further back.

2 See the Armistice Agreement between Jordan and Israel of 1948–9.

3 This view was expressed by King Hussein in an interview with Avi Shlaim, in Ascot, 1996, cited in Shlaim 2001.

4 For example, the US congress refused to supply Jordan with arms (Queen Noor 2003). Jordan sought Arab support, granted in the Baghdad 1979 Arab Summit in the form of an Arab pledge to provide Jordan with financial aid.

5 The US Congress approved US$90,000,000 for that purpose of the proposed US$1.5 billion.

6 See King's interview with Avi Shlaim in Ascot, 1996 (Shlaim 2001).

7 It should be noted that the USSR did admit to Israel's right to existence and made this point of contradiction in view between it and its Arab allies known.

8 The King publicly announced his country's bankruptcy at the Arab Summit held in Baghdad in 1990, obtaining, at the time, formal commitments of aid from Iraq alone upon whom Jordan was growing more dependent. In the mid-1990s trade figures indicated that some 70 per cent of all imports and some 25 per cent of all exports passed through the Jordanian port of Aqaba as transit trade mostly to Iraq (see Markus Bouillon, 'Walking the tightrope' in George Joffé (ed.) (2002: 4)).

9 On 4 August, the Jordanian government announced it would cease to pay salaries of some 18,000 Palestinian civil servants, teachers and health-care workers in the West Bank. The only exceptions were staff of the Ministry of Religious Endowment and Religious Affairs (see the official Jordanian press at the time).

10 Hamas was a movement founded by Sheikh Ahmed Yassin, a paralysed religious teacher, as a wing of the long-standing Muslim Brothers in Palestine. It became the new competitor for the PLO given its massive popularity in the West Bank and Gaza.

11 Rabin, Peres and Yossi Beilin (deputy foreign minister then belonging to the 'extreme dovish wing' of the Labour Party) are the three men primarily responsible for its realization. Secret talks were held for an eight-month period behind a thick veil of secrecy in Oslo, Norway, where Norwegian foreign affairs minister Johan Holst and social scientist Terje Larsen acted as generous hosts and facilitators.

12 Article 25 of the Palestine Mandate, 23 September 1994 in Geopolitics and International Boundaries Research Centre, SOAS, The Final Report on Jordan's Western Boundary, p. 53

13 See the Treaty of Peace, Article 3: International Boundary, Annex 1 (a).

14 Treaty of Peace, Annex II, Article I, Point 3.

15 See the Treaty of Peace's Article 8, Refugees and Displaced Persons, point 2, which speaks of the need to resolve the refugee issue in accordance with international law.

16 The term was coined in 1885 by Nathan Birnbaum, a Jewish Viennese writer, who took it from Zion, one of the biblical names of Jerusalem.

17 The session in question was the forum for historic declarations. A declaration of independence with Jerusalem as the capital (based on UN General Assembly resolution 181 of 1947 advocating the principle of partition) and a call for an international peace

conference based on UN Security Council Resolution 242 guaranteeing Palestinian people's right to self-determination and a rejection of terrorism in all its forms.

18 It is noteworthy, however, that the Palestinians complained of disenfranchisement. For details, see Robins 2004 and Massad 2001.

19 See the Jordanian–Israeli Treaty of Peace, Preamble; Article 2, General Principles; and Article 4, Security.

20 This was confirmed to the author during various interviews with members of the Jordanian top-level leadership in Oxford and Amman in 2004.

21 Note that Hamas shares the same views, being the Muslim Brotherhood's arm in the Occupied Territories. Not surprisingly, its leaders voiced these beliefs upon assuming power in the Occupied Territories following their victory over Fatah in 2006.

3 Achieving and building peace (1994–2003)

1 The famous Syrian poet, Nizar Qabbani, coined a term following the handshake between Arafat and Rabin, *al muharwaluun* (meaning those who scurry/rush), and made it the title of a famous poem which criticized peace and its makers.

2 See, for example, *The Jordan Times'* main editorials after the event. Dr. Walid Sadi (human rights activist, former ambassador and high-ranking official) summed up the popular view at the time saying:

What worries me is the inevitable conclusion that even many moderate Arabs are beginning to share, the idea that peace between Israel and the Arab peoples is unnatural and what is natural is the continuation of a state of war notwithstanding all the peace treaties that have been concluded

(*The Jordan Times*, 22 April 1996).

3 Avi Shlaim: 'His Royal Shyness: King Hussein and Israel', *The New York Review of Books*, 15 July 1999, p. 19

4 For full text of the King's letter to Netanyahu, see *The Jordan Times*, 12 March 1997.

5 For full text of Netanyahu's letter to the King, see *The Jordan Times*, 13 March 1997.

6 See Treaty of Peace document, Article 4, point 5a.

7 For a commentary on the history of peace movements at the macro and micro levels in Israel, see Colin Knox and Padraic Quirk (2000), *Peace Building in Northern Ireland, Israel and South Africa: Transition, Transformation and Reconciliation* (Palgrave), pp. 86–142.

8 See Barry Rubin, *Middle East Review of International Affairs*, Volume 3, no. 4, 1999.

9 See, for example, Avi Shlaim: 'The rise and fall of the Oslo peace process' (Fawcett 2005).

10 For details, see ICG, Middle East Report no. 2, 2002 which also quotes Mohammad Dahlan saying that Bush's demand for a *coup d'état* against Arafat has raised the latter's popularity in the Occupied Territories (ibid.: 2).

11 See the Treaty of Peace, article 6 and Annex no. II.

12 Smadi M., (1998) 'Follow-up report on the trade and economic cooperation agreement between Jordan and Israel', Peace follow-up unit, (RSS, p. 11); Shaqran *et al.* (1998): '*Al Aqabat allati Tuwajih Al Musaddereen min al Urdun ila Israel wa Al Sulta Al Wataniyah Al Filastinyah*' (i.e. Obstacles facing Jordanian exports to Israel and the PNA'), Peace Follow-up Unit, (RSS, p. 18), in Arabic.

13 Quoted in *The Jordan Times*, 15 May 1999, p. 3

14 Smadi 1998: 10; Shaqran *et al.* 1998.
15 See UNDP Human Development Report: 2004, pp. 94-5
16 See for example, Yitzhak Gal: 'Israeli–Jordanian economic relations, 1994–2004', in addition to Khasawneh and Khouri 2002.

4 Obstacles to a warm peace at the structural level

1 The chapter builds on an earlier article by the author entitled 'The first decade of the Jordanian–Israeli peace-building experience: a story of Jordanian challenges (1994–2003)' published in the *Middle East Review of International Affairs* (MERIA) Journal, volume 10, no. 4, article 5/7, December 2006, published by the Global Research in International Affairs (GLORIA) Centre. To read it, visit http://meria.idc.ac.il/journal/2006/issue4/jv10no4a5.html. To read all issues, visit http//:meria.idc.ac.il/
2 Professor Joel Beinin of Stanford University argues that between 2002 and 2003 alone 56 new settlements were established (*Middle East Report Online*, 31 December 2003).
3 Hamas (Arabic for zeal, acronym for Islamic Resistance Movement) was founded in 1987 originally as a religious group of social interests. At first, the Israeli government saw Hamas's non-harmful origins and emergence as a way to weaken the PLO. However, following the Intifada in the 1980s, Hamas changed directions, forming militant wings (Iz Eddin Al Qassam). Hamas's charter clearly states that the movement is 'one of the Muslim Brotherhood wings in Palestine'.
4 Islamic Jihad is a much smaller group with a weaker influence and outreach. It claimed 4–5 per cent of the people's vote in 1996.
5 'Arming the arsonists: Peres, Hamas and the PLO,' available online at: http:www.freeman.org/m_online/apr96/beresa.htm, accessed on 2 November 2003.
6 As cited in the *Jerusalem Post* of 13 September 1995.
7 For details on the story, see the front page of *al-Rai* newspaper of 5 January 2002.
8 In his book *The Missing Peace*, Dennis Ross holds that Arafat condoned the violence erupting with the Second Intifada to boost his negotiation position over the Noble Sanctuary (Al-Haram Al Sharif).
9 Details on the attacks figure in the Jordanian dailies of the period, however, a summary of the main attacks, in English, can be found in Fraser 2004, pp. 159–174.
10 See ICG, Middle East Report no. 1 published in 2002.
11 Gary Sussman quotes figures provided by Sharon's advisers on the number of settlers to be relocated from the West Bank indicating the withdrawal plan to be along the 1967 Yigal Allon, plan which would ensure Israeli control over significant portions of the West Bank, leaving the Palestinians roughly 58 per cent of the territories, (*Middle East Report Online,* March, 2005).
12 See ICG Report: 'Middle East Endgame I', Middle East Report No. 2, 2002.
13 For an elaboration on the concept of BATNA see Fisher and Ury (1981).
14 See ICG interview, ME report no. 22, pp. 22–23
15 US direct intervention in the region has grown after the cold war. Unlike the 1957 Eisenhower and 1980 Carter doctrines whereby state sovereignty was largely honoured (L. Carl Brown 2004: VIII), the events of 11 September 2001 granted the United States rights to the detriment of state sovereignty. To many in the region, this was a new form of imperialism, an imposition of external will, reviving the Ottoman syndrome.
16 Following the bombing of two buses in Jerusalem, for example, *The Jordan Times'* issue of 4 March 1996 opened with 'the bombs are aimed at peace'.

17 See for example *The Jordan Times* of 20 April 1996
18 See for example, Michael Herzog; Gal, Yitzhak and David Makovsky: 'Peace Pays Off for Jordan', *Los Angeles Times*, 31 January 2003, available online from the Washington Institute for Near East Policy; also see Rosenberg 2003: 126–7.
19 See Markus Bouillon in Joffé, ed. 2002
20 See World Bank's report entitled: 'Peace and the Jordanian economy', 1994, The International Bank for Reconstruction and Development
21 Annual US funding levels to Jordan have increased dramatically, from US$7.2 million in fiscal year 1996 to more than US$126 million in 1997, US$140 million in 1998, and a continued average of US$200 million per year in the following years through 2003 (USAID.gov website).
22 See *Middle East International*, 10 December 1999 and UNDP Jordan development Report, 2004, available online at www.undp-jordan.org/JordanHumanDevelopment Report/tabid/81/Default.aspx.
23 According to Herzog, 2004, Jordanian exports to the US increased from US$16 million in 1998 to US$670 million in 2003. Given Jordan's gross domestic product of approximately US$9.8 billion and less than US$3 billion in annual exports, this is a major boon to the country's economy.
24 While the real GDP per capita rose from US$ 3,450 in 1997 to US$4,129 in 2002 (i.e. an increase of nearly 20 per cent over the five-year period), in 1993 real GDP per capita was actually US$4,380, indicating that the standard of living was not necessarily improving over time.
25 For an explanation of the concept and role of non-violent action as a technique of struggle, see, for example, Jeong, Ho-Won, ed., (1999) *The New Agenda for Peace Research*, (Ashgate Publishing), pp. 33–5.
26 The 'anti-normalization committee' (one of the committees within the professional associations) was established following the signing of the peace treaty in 1994. Each of the 14 associations had at least one representative within the committee which held weekly meetings and made recommendations issued later as directives to all association members and partners (e.g. engineering and contracting companies, etc.) by the Council of Association Presidents (*majlis al-nuqaba*). The latter consisted of the 14 presidents of the 14 associations in the complex. 'Recommendations' were in essence orders for boycott of a particular individual or company (i.e. normalizers) or product.
27 For more information on Jordanian political parties see Hani Hourani's (1997) *Jordanian Political Parties* (Amman: al-Urdun al-Jadid Research Centre and Sinbad Publishing House). For more information on the Leftist movement in Jordan, see Sami al-Khazendar's (1997) *Jordan and the Palestine Question: The Role of Islamic and Left Forces in Foreign Policy Making* (Reading: Ithaca Press).
28 For example, attending the Copenhagen peace conference was reason, in 2001, for blacklisting Adnan Abu Odeh and former Prime Minister and Chief of the Royal Court Fayez Tarawneh.
29 While one generic anti-normalization committee served all the associations, the engineering association had its own internal anti-normalization committee, making it necessary to study the engineers' association by-laws in particular.
30 See *al-Rai* newspaper of 2 December 2002.
31 *Al-Majd* newspaper published on 3 January 2001 a *fatwa* (Islamic interpretation) by Sheikh Yousef Qardawi calling for the boycott of US and Israeli products as a Muslim

duty. The anti-normalization movement in 2002 seconded the appeal to boycott a long detailed list of US and Israeli products available in the market, including candy, snacks, soft drinks, personal care items, foodstuff, detergents, vehicles and every commodity of US or Israeli source or origin. Substitutes were listed. As a result, the anti-normalization committee president, Abul Sukkar, was arrested on 7 October 2002 on charges of damaging the economy.

32 For example: 'Our culture in face of normalization' (*Thaqafatuna fi muwajahat al-tatbee'*) on 10 July 1993, 'Peace and what is after peace' (*al-salam wa ma ba'd al-salam*) on 18 September 1993, a seminar and public debate entitled 'our culture in face of normalization' (*Thaqafatuna fi muwajahat al-tatbee'*) on 27 March 1994, 'the anti-normalization experience in Egypt' (*tajribat muwajahat al-tatbee' fi masr*) on 19 July 1994 and 'Does Israel really want normalization?' (*hal tureed Israeli haqqan al-tatbee'*) on 15 January 1995.

33 *The Jordan Times'* front page of 18 May 1999, said that Barak's election was 'the last chance to salvage the battered Middle East peace process'.

5 The refugee question and peace

1 For more on the issue, see Said, Edward, *Peace and Its Discontents: Gaza–Jericho 1993–1995*, (1995).

2 See International Crisis Group Report: 'Palestinian Refugees and the Politics of Peacemaking', Middle East Report no. 22, 5 February 2004.

3 See ICG, Middle East Report no. 22, 2004.

4 UNRWA, the international agency responsible for the provision of relief services for the Palestinian refugees since 1950, counted, as of 1 March 2003, 4.1 million refugee beneficiaries (including descendants) in its areas of operation, of whom 1.7 million (42 per cent) were reported in Jordan. Some might argue that the figures of UNRWA are not accurate as they only count those eligible beneficiaries as refugees and exclude Palestinians with no residency rights in their areas of operations, those removed from their rolls over the years for various reasons and those who never registered with the organization in the first place. Nonetheless, the figures may be considered comprehensive enough as they include those who no longer live in refugee camps but are UNRWA-registered and which make up two thirds of the refugees counted.

5 See the Palestinian Centre for Policy and Survey Research's website at http://www. pcpsr.org/

6 In April, 2004, President Bush Jr. exchanged letters with Sharon in which he agreed that the return of the refugees (whose numbers ranged between 4 to 6 million) will never happen; declaring as well that the 1949 armistice line was no longer a realistic boundary for Israel given other realities on the ground. This marked a departure from US policies backing Resolution 242, which enshrined the inadmissibility of land acquisition by force while also weakening the prospects of a viable Palestinian state already threatened by territorial inadequacy.

7 See the Jordanian–Israeli Treaty of Peace, Preamble, Article 2, General Principles and Article 4, Security.

8 See: 'Sharon's unilateral steps', *Middle East Report Online*, 31 December 2003.

6 Leaderships and the peacebuilding process

1 King Hussein would constantly address the Jordanian people as 'the best of families and the best of tribes' as well as his 'clan'.
2 See the Speech from the Throne at the opening of the thirteenth Parliament, 29 November 1997
3 Not surprisingly, Jordan immediately sent an ambassador to Israel in early 2005 when signs of Palestinian–Israeli progress were visible under the new Palestinian leadership.
4 Shaqran *et al.* (1998), 'Obstacles facing Jordanian exporters to Israel and the Palestinian authority', (UNDP-RSS).
5 For more information, see the report by Ahmad Shaqran, Yazan Bakhit and Tal'at B'dour (1998), 'Obstacles facing Jordanian exports to Israel and the Palestinian authority', (Royal Scientific Society, UNDP), Arabic.

7 The road to a warm peace

1 See for example, Sameeh Ma'aitah: 'The 'substitute homeland' and Security threats persist despite a Peace Treaty and Normalization', *Al Arab Al Yaoum*, 2 March, 1998 (Arabic).
2 Tami Steinmetz Centre for Peace Research, *peace index*, December 2000
3 More comforting to Likud members were the declarations that any negotiations likely to be on a Palestinian state would first be discussed and approved by Sharon's government which included members of the two parties mostly opposed to such a prospect: the National Religious Party and the National Union Party.

Bibliography

Official speeches and remarks

Various speeches of King Abdullah II, 1999–2003, available online at www.kingabdullah.jo
Various speeches of King Hussein, 1994–9, available online at www.kinghussein.gov.jo/
library.html
Various speeches of Prince Hassan, 1994–9, available online at www.elhassan.org

Documents and official publications

Constitution of the Hashemite Kingdom of Jordan, available online at http://www.kinghus-
sein.gov.jo/constitution_jo.html.
Geopolitics and International Boundaries Research Centre (1994) *Final Report on Jordan's
Western Boundary,* London: SOAS.
Jordanian–Israeli Treaty of Peace (26 October 1994), available online at http://www.incore.
ulst.ac.uk/services/cds/agreements/israel-jordan.html.
Jordanian Ministry of Water and Irrigation (2003) The National Water Master Plan of
Jordan .
Ministry of Education, Jordan (first printed in 1994, reprinted in 1995, 1996, 1997, 1998,
1999) *Jordan's Geography,* tenth Grade, (scientific editor Musa Shihab).
—— (first printed in 1994, reprinted in 1995, 1996, 1997) *Modern Arab History and
Contemporary Issues*, Part II, tenth grade school textbook.
—— (First edition in 1994, reprinted in 1995 and 2003) *National and Civil Education,*
tenth grade, (scientific editor Dr. Musa Abu Sil).
Ministry of Foreign Affairs, Israel (13 September 1993) 'The Declaration of Principles
on Interim Self-Government Arrangements', available online at http://www.mfa.gov.il/
MFA/Peace+Process/Guide+to+the+Peace+Process/Declaration+of+Principles.htm.
Mitchell Commission Report (Sharm al Shaikh fact-finding Committee), Full text of
the report completed on April 30, 2001, and published on May 20, 2001, Wash-
ington, DC.
UNDP, Ministry of Planning and International Cooperation of Jordan and the United
Nations Development Programme (2004) 'Jordan Human Development Report 2004:
Building Sustainable Livelihoods'.

UNRWA Newsletter (1987) 'The Average Palestine Refugee,' in *Palestine Refugees Today*, 117, Vienna, January.

Washington Institute for Near East Policy Hamas (2002) 'The Fundamentalist Challenge to the PLO, Executive Summary', available online at http://www.washingtoninstitute.org (accessed 2 November 2003)

Unpublished works

Cunningham, William G. (1998) 'Theoretical Framework for Conflict Resolution, Conflict Theory and the Conflict in Northern Ireland', unpublished MA thesis, University of Auckland.

Fisher, Franklin et al. (2000) 'Optimal Water Management and Conflict Resolution: The Middle East Water Project', Revised Draft.

Kraybill, S. (1996) 'An Anabaptist Paradigm for Conflict Transformation: Critical Reflections on Peacemaking in Zimbabwe', unpublished D. Phil. Dissertation, Department of Religious Studies, University of Cape Town, South Africa.

Mango, Adiba (2003) 'Jordan on the Road to Peace, 1988–1999', unpublished D.Phil. thesis, University of Oxford.

Warnes, Kevin Robert 'West European Foreign and Security Policy-Making, National Interests and Regional Cooperation (1990–1994)', unpublished D.Phil. thesis, University of Bradford.

Books and articles

Abbas, M. (1995) *Through Secret Channels: The Road to Oslo*, Reading, UK: Garnet Publishing.

Abootalebi, A. (1998) 'Civil Society, Democracy and the Middle East', *Middle East Review of International Affairs*, 2(3).

Abu-Nimer, M. (ed.) (2001) *Reconciliation, Justice and Coexistence, Theory and Practice*, Lexington Books.

Abu-Odeh, A. (1999) *Jordanians, Palestinians, and the Hashemite Kingdom of Jordan in the Middle East Peace Process*, Washington, DC: United States Institute of Peace Press.

Aggestam, K. (1999) '*Reframing and Resolving Conflict: Israeli–Palestinian Negotiations 1988–1998*', Lund University Press.

Aghabi, F. (1999) 'Follow-up Report on the Tourism Cooperation Agreement between Jordan and Israel in the Treaty of Peace', Royal Scientific Society and UNDP.

Al-Ahmad, N. (1999) 'Follow-Up Report on the Transport Agreement between Jordan and Israel in the Treaty of Peace', Royal Scientific Society–UNDP (Arabic).

Al-Khazendar, S. (1997) *Jordan and the Palestine Question: The Role of Islamic and Left Forces in Foreign Policy Making*, Reading: Ithaca Press.

Allen, L. (2003) 'Uncertainty and Disquiet Mark Intifada's Third Anniversary', Middle East Research and Information Project, *Middle East Report Online*.

Almaani, W. (1998) 'Follow-up Report on the Scientific and Cultural Cooperation Agreement between Jordan and Israel in the Treaty of Peace: Technical Support for Jordan's Role in the Middle East Peace Process', RSS–UNDP.

Andoni, L. (1995) 'Hussein's Toughest Dilemma', *Middle East International*, 26 May.

—— (1999) 'Amman "new political thinking"', *Middle East International*, 26 November.

Antoun, R. (1997) 'Institutionalised deconfrontation: A Case Study of Conflict Resolution among Tribal Peasants in Jordan', in Salem, Paul (ed.), *Conflict Resolution in the Arab World: Selected Essays*, American University of Beirut.

Aruri, N. (1972) *Jordan: A Study in Political Development, 1921–1965*, The Hague: Martinus Nijhoff.

Assefa, H. (2001) 'Coexistence and Reconciliation in the Northern Region of Ghana', in Abu-Nimer M. (ed.) *Reconciliation, Justice and Coexistence, Theory and Practice*, Lexington Books.

Avruch, K. (2002) *Culture and Conflict Resolution*, United States Institute of Peace Press, 3rd printing.

Azar, E (1991) 'The Analysis and Management of Protracted Conflicts,' in Vamik, D. Volkan, J. Montville, V. and Julius, D. (eds) (1991) *The Psychodynamics of International Relationships*, Vol. 2, Lexington, MA: Lexington.

Badran, I. (1999) 'Follow-up Report on the Agreement for the Implementation of Article 19 (Energy) between Jordan and Israel in the Treaty of Peace', RSS–UNDP.

Bailey, Clinton (1984) *Jordan's Palestinian Challenge, 1948–1983: A Political History*, Colorado: Westview Press

Bar, Shmuel (1995) 'The Jordanian Elite – Change and Continuity' in Susser A.and Shmuelevitz A. (eds) *The Hashemites in the Modern Arab World*, Frank Cass & Co. Ltd.

Barari, H. (2004) *Jordan and Israel, Ten Years Later*, Centre for Strategic Studies.

Bar'el, Z. (1999) 'Who Arab Leaders Are Voting For', *Ha'aretz,* 2 May 1999.

BBC news online, 'Hamas Chief Killed in Air Strike', 22 March 2004.

Beinin, J. (2003) 'Sharon's Unilateral Steps', *Middle East Report Online*, 31 December 2003.

Bennis, W. (1999) 'The End of Leadership', Centre for the Advanced Study of Leadership Selected Proceedings, 1998 Annual Meeting: Leaders/Scholars Association, The James MacGregor Burns Academy of Leadership.

Bercovitch, J. (1997) 'Mediation in International Conflict: An Overview of Theory, A Review of Practice', in Zartman I. and Rasmussen J. (eds) *Peacemaking in International Conflict: Methods and Techniques*, Washington DC: United States Press Institute of Peace.

Binder, L. (ed.) (1999) *Ethnic Conflict and International Politics in the Middle East*, University Press of Florida.

Bligh, A. (2000), *The Political Legacy of King Hussein,* Sussex Academic Press.

—— (2001) 'The Jordanian Army: Between Domestic and External Challenges', *Middle East Review of International Affairs*, 5(2).

Bloomfield, D. (1997a) *Peacemaking Strategies in Northern Ireland: Building Complementarity in Conflict Management Theory*, London: Macmillan.

—— (1997b) *Resolution and Settlement Approaches*, London: Macmillan.

Bloomfield, D., Barnes, T. and Huyse, L. (eds) (2003) *Reconciliation After Violent Conflict, a Handbook*, International Institute for Democracy and Electoral Assistance.

Boulding, E. and Boulding, K. (1995) *The Future Images and Processes,* Sage Publications.

Boulding, K. (1962) *Conflict and Defense*, New York: Harper and Row.

Brand, L. (1994) *Jordan's Inter-Arab Relations: The Political Economy of Alliance Making*, Columbia University Press.

—— (1995) 'Palestinian and Jordanians: A crisis of identity', *Journal of Palestinian Studies* 24(4): 36.

—— (1999) 'Al-Muhajirin w-al-Ansar: Hashemite Strategies for Managing Communal Identity in Jordan' in Binder, L. (ed.) *Ethnic Conflict and International Politics in the Middle East*, University Press of Florida.

—— (2004) 'In Search of Budget Security: A Re-examination of Jordanian Foreign Policy' in Brown, C. L. (ed.) *Diplomacy in the Middle East: The International Relations of Regional and Outside Powers*, I. B. Tauris.

Braumoeller, B. (2003) 'A Dynamic Solution to the Agent–Structure Debate in International Relations', paper presented at CEEISA/ISA International Convention, Budapest, Hungary.

Braybrooke, D. and Lindblom, C. (1963) *A Strategy of Decision: Policy Evaluation as a Social Process*, New York: The Free Press.

Brickell, David (2001) *Leadership for Poverty Reduction: Public and Private Leadership*, United Nations University, Leadership Academy.

Brown, C. (2001) *Understanding International Relations*, 2nd edn, Palgrave.

Brown, L.C. (ed.) (2004) *Diplomacy in the Middle East: The International Relations of Regional and Outside Powers*, I. B. Tauris & Co. Ltd.

Burchill, S., Devetak, R., Linklater, A., Paterson, M., Reus-Smit, C. and True, J. (2001) *Theories of International Relations*, 2nd edn, Palgrave.

Burns, M. J. (1978) *Leadership*, New York: Harper & Row.

—— (2003) *Transforming Leadership*, New York: Atlantic Monthly Press.

Burton, J. (1987) *Resolving Deep-rooted conflicts : A Handbook*, Lanham, MD: University Press of America.

—— (1990a) *Conflict Resolution and Provention*, New York: St. Martin's Press, Inc.

—— (1990b) 'Conflict: Human Needs Theory', Vol. 2 of the Conflict series, London: Macmillan.

Carlsnaes, W. (1994) 'In Lieu of a Conclusion: Compatibility and the Agency–Structure Issue in Foreign Policy Analysis,' in Carlsnaes, W. and Smith, S. (eds) *European Foreign Policy. The EC and Changing Perspectives in Europe,* London: Sage Publications.

Carr, E. (1961) *What is History?*, New York: Vintage books.

Chemers, M. and Roya, A. (eds) (1993) *Leadership Theory and Research: Perspectives and Directions*, San Diego: Academic Press.

Chomsky, N. (2003) *Middle East Illusions: Including Peace in the Middle East? Reflections on Justice and Nationhood*, Rowan & Littlefield Publishers, Inc.

Ciulla, J. B. (1998) *Ethics, The Heart of Leadership,* Westport, CT: Praeger Publishers.

Cohen, R. (1990) *Culture and Conflict in the Egyptian–Israeli Relations: A dialogue of the Deaf*, Bloomington, IN: Indiana University Press.

Cook, J. (2003) 'Declining to Intervene: Israel's Supreme Court and the Occupied Territories', Middle East Research and Information Project, *Middle East Report Online*, 4 August.

Cousens, E., Kumar, C. and Wermester, K. (eds) (2001) *Peacebuilding as Politics, Cultivating Peace in Fragile Societies*, Boulder, CO: Lynne Reinner Publishers.

Couto, R., and Richard, A. (1999) 'To Give Their Gifts: The Innovative, Transforming Leadership of Adaptive Work', Centre for the Advanced Study of Leadership Selected Proceedings, 1998 Annual Meeting: Leaders/Scholars Association, The James MacGregor Burns Academy of Leadership, 1999.

Crabtree, B. F. and Miller, W. L. (1992) *Doing Qualitative Research*, Newbury Park, CA: Sage.

Crawley, J. (1992) *Constructive Conflict Management*, London: Nicholas Brealey Publishing.

Dallas, R. (1999) *King Hussein: A Life on the Edge*, New York: Fromm International Edition.

Deutsch, K., Merritt, R. and Kelman, H. (1965) 'Effects of Events on National and International Images' in Deutsch, K., Merritt, R. and Kelman, H. (eds) *International Behavior: A Social–Psychological Analysis*, New York: Holt, Rinehart and Winston Inc.

Deutsch, M. (1991) 'Subjective Features of Conflict Resolution: Psychological, Social and Cultural Features', in Vayrynen, R. (ed.) *New Directions in Conflict Theory: Conflict Resolution and Conflict Transformation*, London: Sage.

Edinger, L. J. (1990) 'Approaches to the Comparative Analysis of Political Leadership', in *Review of Politics*, 54(4): 520.

El-Naser, H. (1998) 'Follow-up Report on the Water Agreement between Jordan and Israel in the Treaty of Peace', RSS–UNDP.

El-Samen, T. (1998) 'Follow-up Report on the Agreement on Cooperation in the fields of Health and Medicine between Jordan and Israel in the Treaty of Peace', RSS–UNDP.

Estrada-Hollenbeck, M. (2001) 'The Attainment of Justice through Restoration, Not Litigation: The Subjective Road to Reconciliation', in Abu-Nimer M. (ed.) *Reconciliation, Justice and Coexistence, Theory and Practice*, Lexington Books.

Farnham, B. (1990) 'Political Cognition and Decision-Making', *Political Psychology* 11(1): 83–111.

Fetherston, A. B. and Parkin, A. C. (1997) 'Transforming Violent Conflict: Contributions from Social Theory', in Broadhead, L. A. (ed.) *Issues in Peace Research 1997–1998, Theory and Practice*, University of Bradford.

Fisher, R. and Ury, W. (1981) *Getting to Yes*, Boston, MA: Houghton Mifflin.

—— (1991) *Getting to Yes: Negotiating Agreement without giving in*, New York: Penguin Books.

Fisher, R.J. (2001) 'Social–Psychological Processes in Interactive Conflict Analysis and Reconciliation', in Abu-Nimer, M. (ed.) *Reconciliation, Justice and Coexistence, Theory and Practice*, Lexington Books.

Fitzduff, M. (2001) 'The Challenge to History: Justice, Coexistence, and Reconciliation Work in Northern Ireland' in Abu-Nimer, M. (ed.) *Reconciliation, Justice and Coexistence, Theory and Practice*, Lexington Books.

Fraser, T.G. (2004) *The Arab–Israeli Conflict*, 2nd edn, Palgrave Macmillan.

Fruchter-Ronen, I. (2004) 'The Idea of the "Alternative Homeland" and the Process of the Consolidation of Jordanian National Identity: The Role of the Israeli–Jordanian Peace Agreement in this Process', paper presented at the international conference 'Israel–Jordan Relations: The First Decade of Formal Peace 1994–2004', Haifa University, 5–8 December 2004.

Gal, Y. (2004) 'Israeli–Jordanian Economic Relations 1994–2004', paper presented at the international conference 'Israel–Jordan Relations: The First Decade of Formal Peace 1994–2004', Haifa University, 5–8 December 2004.

Galtung, J. (1975) 'Three Approaches to peace: Peacekeeping, Peacemaking and Peace-building' in Galtung, J. *Peace, War and Defence, Essays in Peace Research Vol. 2*, Copenhagen: Christian Ejlers, pp. 282–304.

—— (2001) 'After Violence, Reconstruction, Reconciliation, and Resolution: Coping with Visible and Invisible Effects of War and Violence' in Abu-Nimer, M. (ed.) *Reconciliation, Justice and Coexistence, Theory and Practice*, Lexington Books.

Galtung, J. and Jacobsen, C. (2000) *Searching for Peace, the Road to Transcend*, London: Pluto Press.

Gardner, J. W. (1990) *On Leadership*, New York: The Free Press.

Gordhan, P. (2000) 'Political Leadership in Divided Societies: The Case of South African Experience' INCORE conference papers. Available online at http://www.incore.ulst.ac.uk.

Green, J. (1997) 'Ideology and Conflict in Arab Politics', in Salem, P. (ed.) *Conflict Resolution in the Arab World: Selected Essays,* American University of Beirut.

Greenwood, S. (2003) 'Jordan's "New Bargain": The Political Economy of Regime Security', *Middle East Journal*, 57(2).

Guzzini, S. (2000) 'A Reconstruction of Constructivism in International Relations', *European Journal of International Relations*, 6(2): 147–82.

Haddad, S. (2003) *The Palestinian Impasse in Lebanon, The Politics of Refugee Integration*, Sussex Academic Press.

Halaiqah, M. (1999) 'Follow-up Report on the Qualifying Industrial Zone', RSS–UNDP.

Hampson, F. O. (1996) *Nurturing Peace*, United States Institute of Peace Press.

Hattar, N. (2003a) *The Jordanian Elite and Issues of Modernisation and Democracy*, Azminah (Arabic).

—— (2003b) *Neo-Liberalism in Face of Democracy: Readings in the Jordanian Case Study*, Azminah (Arabic).

Haugerudbraaten, H. (1998) 'Peacebuilding: Six Dimensions and two Concepts', in *African Security Review*, 7(6).

Hauss, C. (2001) *International Conflict Resolution: International Relations for the 21st Century*, Continuum.

Hawatmeh, G. (ed.) (1995) *The Role of the Media in a Democracy: the Case of Jordan*, University of Jordan, Centre for Strategic Studies.

Heifetz, R. A. (1994) *Leadership Without Easy Answers*, Cambridge, MA: Belknap/Harvard University Press

—— (1999) 'Staying Alive', Centre for the Advanced Study of Leadership Selected Proceedings, 1998 Annual Meeting: Leaders/Scholars Association, The James MacGregor Burns Academy of Leadership.

Heradstveit, D. (1979) *The Arab Israeli Conflict: Psychological obstacles to peace*, Oslo: Universitetsforlaget.

Herzog, M. (2004) 'A Decade of Israeli–Jordanian Peace: An untold Economic Success Story', Peace Watch Report no. 478, The Washington Institute for Near East Policy.

Hinnebusch, R. (2003) *The International Politics of the Middle East*, Manchester University Press.

—— (2005) 'Explaining International Politics in the Middle East: The Struggle of Regional Identity and Systemic Structure', in Gerd Nonneman (ed.) *Analysing Middle East Foreign Policies, and the Relationship with Europe*, Oxon: Routledge.

Hodgkinson, C. (1983) *The Philosophy of Leadership*, Oxford: Blackwell.

Hollander, E. P. (1993) 'Legitimacy, Power, and Influence: A Perspective on Relational Features of Leadership', in Chemers, M. and Ayman R. (eds) *Leadership Theory and Research*, Academic Press.

Hollis, M. and Smith, S. (1990) *Explaining and Understanding International Relations*, Oxford: Oxford University Press.

Holsti, O. R. (1962) 'The Belief System and National Images' in *International Studies Quarterly*, 13(4): 190–222.

Hourani, H. (1997) *Jordanian Political Parties,* Amman: al-Urdun al-Jadid Research Centre and Sinbad Publishing House.

Hourani, H. and Abu-Rumman, H. (eds) (1996) *The Democratic Process in Jordan ... Where to?,* Al-Urdun Al-Jadid Research Centre.

International Crisis Group, 'A Time to Lead: The International Community and the Israeli–Palestinian Conflict', Middle East Report no. 1, 10 April 2002. Available online at www.icg.org.

—— 'Middle East Endgame I: Getting to a Comprehensive Arab–Israeli Peace Settlement', Middle East Report No. 2, 16 July 2002. Available online at www.icg.org.

—— 'Dealing with Hamas', Middle East Report no. 21, 26 January 2004. Available online at www.icg.org.

—— 'Palestinian Refugees and the Politics of Peacemaking', Middle East Report no. 22, 5 February 2004. Available online at www.icg.org.

—— 'Identity Crisis: Israel and its Arab Citizens', Middle East Report No. 25, 4 March 2004. Available online at www.icg.org.

Irani, G. E. (1999) 'Islamic Mediation Techniques for Middle East Conflicts', *Middle East Review of International Affairs*, 3(2).

Jamil, A. and Khasawneh, M. (1999) 'Follow-up Report on the Memorandum of Understanding Concerning Cooperation in the Field of Telecommunications and Posts between Jordan and Israel in the Treaty of Peace', UNDP–RSS.

Janis, I., Smith, B. and Kelman, H. (1965) 'Effects of Education and Persuasion on National and International Images', in Janis, I., Smith B. and Kelman H. (eds) *International Behaviour: A Social–Psychological Analysis*, Holt, Rinehart and Winston Inc.

Jeong, H. W. (ed.) (1999) *The New Agenda for Peace Research*, Ashgate Publishing.

—— (2000) *Peace and Conflict Studies: An Introduction*, Ashgate Publishing.

Joffé, G. (ed.) (2002) *Jordan in Transition,* Hurst & Company.

Kavaloski, V.C. (1990) 'Transactional Citizen Peacemaking as Nonviolent Action', *Peace and Change,* 15(2).

Kelman, H. (ed.) (1965) *International Behaviour: A Social–Psychological Analysis*, Holt, Rinehart and Winston Inc.

—— (1999) 'Transforming the Relationship between Former Enemies: A Social–psychological analysis', in Rothstein, R. (ed.) *After the Peace: Resistance and Reconciliation,* London: Lynne Rienner.

Kennedy, G. and Williams, C. (eds) (2002) 'Be Able to Hope: An Interview with Thorvald Stoltenberg', United Nations University.

Khasawneh, M. (1998) 'Follow-up Report on the Agricultural Agreement between Jordan and Israel in the Treaty of Peace', RSS–UNDP.

Khasawneh, M. and Khouri, R. (2002) *The US–Jordan Free Trade Agreement and Qualifying Industrial Zones as a Model for Industrial Development: The Case of Jordan and its Implication for the Middle East Region,* RSS & Friedrich Ebert Stiftung

Khuri, F. (1997) 'The Ascent to Top Office in Arab–Islamic Culture: A Challenge to Democracy,' in Paul, S. (ed.) *Conflict Resolution in the Arab World: Selected Essays,* American University of Beirut.

Kilani, S. (1998) 'Black Year for Democracy in Jordan', Euro-Mediterranean Human Rights Network, Arab Archives Institute.

—— (2002) *Press Freedoms in Jordan,* Euro-Mediterranean Human Rights Network, Arab Archives Institute.

Klein, M. (1995) 'Focus on Hamas: The PLO's Friend or Foe?', online article accessed on 2 November 2003, www.ict.org.il/articles/articledet.cfm?articleid=89.

Knowles, W. (2005) *Jordan since 1989, A Study in Political Economy,* I. B. Tauris.

Knox, C. and Quirk P. (2000) *Peace Building in Northern Ireland, Israel and South Africa: Transition, Transformation and Reconciliation,* Palgrave Macmillan.

Kolb, D. M. and Associates (1994) *When Talk Works: Profiles of Mediators,* San Francisco: Jossey Bass Publishers.

Kriesberg, L., Northrup, T. A. and Thornson, S. J. (eds) (1989) *Intractable Conflicts and Their Transformation,* Syracuse University Press.

—— (1998) *Constructive Conflicts From Escalation to Resolution,* Rowman and Littlefield Publishers.

Kurzman, C. (ed.) (1998) *Liberal Islam: a Sourcebook,* Oxford University Press.

Lalor, P. (1997) 'Black September, White September' paper presented at symposium sponsored by CERMOC, Paris, 24–25 June.

Lederach, J. P. (1995a) *Preparing for Peace. Conflict Transformation across Cultures,* Syracuse University Press.

—— (1995b) 'Beyond Violence: Building Sustainable Peace' in A. Williamson (ed.) *Beyond Violence,* Belfast, Ireland: Community Relations Council.

—— (1997) *Building Peace, Sustainable Reconciliation in Divided Societies,* Washington DC: United States Institute of Peace Press.

Lee, Y.-J. (2004) *Leadership and International Understanding: Linking Korea and the Arab Middle East,* United Nations University.

Lunt, J. (1989) *Hussein of Jordan, Searching for a Just and Lasting Peace: A Political Biography,* Macmillan.

Lynch, M. (1999) *State Interests and public spheres: the international politics of Jordan's identity,* New York: Columbia University Press.

—— (2004) 'No Jordan Option', Middle East Research and Information Project, *Middle East Report online,* 21 June.

McNeil, E. (1965) *The Nature of Human Conflict,* Englewood Cliffs: Prentice-Hall.

Majali, A. S. (2004) *Rihlat al-Umr: min Bayt al-Sha'r Ila Siddat al-Hukm,* Matbu'at llitawzi' wa al-nashr, (Arabic).

Massad, J. (2001) *Colonial Effects: The Making of National Identity in Jordan,* Columbia University Press.

Mayer, B. (2000) *The Dynamics of Conflict Resolution: a Practitioner's Guide,* San Francisco: Josey-Bass Publishers.

Meyer, R. (2001) *Leadership in South Africa: From Dogma to Transformation – An Account of Paradigm Shift,* UN University, Leadership Academy, Occasional Papers, Leaders Series no. 1.

Miall, H. (2003) 'Conflict Transformation: A Multi-Dimensional Task', *Berghof Handbook for Conflict Transformation.* Available online at www.berghof-handbook.net.

Miall, H., Ramsbothan, O. and Woodhouse, T. (1999) *Contemporary Conflict Resolution,* Polity Press.

Moore, P. W. (2003) 'The Newest Jordan: Free Trade, Peace and an Ace in the Hole', *Middle East Report Online,* 26 June.

Nielsen, Jorgen and Khasawneh, Sami (1998) *Arabs and the West: Mutual Images,* Jordan University Press.

Nonneman, G. (2001) 'State of the art Rentiers and Autocrats, Monarch and Democrats, State and Society: the Middle East between Globalization, Human 'agency' and Europe', *International Affairs* 77(I): 141–62.

Noor, Queen (2003) *Leap of Faith: Memoirs of an Unexpected Life,* Weidenfeld & Nicolson.

Orr, A. (1994) *Israel: Politics, Myths and Identity Crises,* Pluto Press.

Patokallio, P. (2004) 'European Union Policy on the Arab–Israeli Conflict: From Prayer to Player', Middle East Paper no. 77, University of Durham, Institute of Middle Eastern and Islamic Studies, December.

Perthes, V. (ed.) (2004) *Arab Elites: Negotiating the Politics of Change,* Lynne Rienner.

Pundak, R. (2001) 'From Oslo to Taba: What Went Wrong?', *Survival,* The International Institute for Strategic Studies, 43(3): 31–45.

Quandt, W. B. (1993) *Peace Process: American Diplomacy and the Arab–Israeli Conflict since 1967,* Washington DC/Berkeley: Brookings/University of California Press.

Rabbani, M. (2003) 'The Road from Aqaba', Middle East Research and Information Project, *Middle East Report online,* 13 June.

Rabinovich, I. (1999) *Waging Peace: Israel and the Arabs at the End of the Century,* New York: Farrar, Straus and Giroux

Rabinovich, I. and Reinharz, J. (eds) (1984) *Israel in the Middle East,* Oxford University Press.

Robins, P. (1998) 'Shedding Half a Kingdom', *British Society for Middle East Studies Bulletin*, 16(2).

—— (2004) *A History of Jordan*, Cambridge: Cambridge University Press.

Rosati, J. A.(1995) 'A Cognitive Approach to the Study of Foreign Policy', in Neack, L., Hey, J. and Haney, P. J. (eds) *Foreign Policy Analysis*, Englewood Cliffs, NJ: Prentice Hall.

Rosenberg, J. M. (2003) *Nation-Building: A Middle East Recovery Program*, University Press of America Inc.

Ross, D. (2004) *The Missing Peace: The Inside Story of the Fight for Middle East Peace*, New York: Farrar, Straus and Giroux

Ross, M. H. (1993) *The Management of Conflict: Interpretations and Interests in Comparative Perspective*, Yale University Press.

Rost, J. (1991) *Leadership for the twenty-first century*, New York: Praeger.

Rubin, B. (1997a) 'Israel, The Palestinian Authority, and the Arab States', *Middle East for Review of International Affairs*, 1(4).

—— (1997b) 'The Politics of the New Middle East', *Middle East Review of International Politics*, 1(3).

Rubin, B. (1999) 'External Factors in Israel's 1999 Elections', *Middle East Review of International Affairs*, 3(4), December.

Rubinstein, E. (1996) 'The Treaty of Peace with Jordan', chapter 47, published in Kaplan, Alon (ed.), *Israeli Business Law*, 559–65, Kluwer Law International.

Said, E. (1995) *Peace and Its Discontents: Gaza–Jericho 1993–1995*, Vintage.

—— (2001) *Reflections on Exile*, Penguin Books.

Salem, P. (ed.) (1997) *Conflict Resolution in the Arab World: Selected Essays*, American University of Beirut.

Salibi, K. (1993) *The Modern History of Jordan*, I. B. Tauris, London.

Sandole, D. (1993) 'Paradigms, Theories and Metaphors in Conflict and Conflict Resolution: Coherence and Confusion?', in Sandole, D. and van der Merwe, H. (eds) *Conflict Resolution Theory and Practice, Integration and Application*, Manchester University Press.

Satloff, R. (1994) *From Abdullah to Hussein: Jordan in Transition*, Oxford University Press.

Scham, P. and Russell, L. (2001) '"Normalization" and "Anti-Normalization" in Jordan: The Public Debate', *Middle East Review of International Affairs*, 5(3).

Shaqran, A., Bakhit, Y. and B'dour, T. (1998) 'Obstacles Facing Jordanian Exports to Israel and the Palestinian Authority', RSS–UNDP (Arabic).

Shlaim, A. (1995) *War and Peace in the Middle East*, Penguin Books.

—— (1999) 'His Royal Shyness: King Hussein and Israel', *The New York Review of Books*, 46(12), 15 July.

—— (2001) *The Iron Wall: Israel and the Arab World*, Norton & Co.

—— (2005) 'The Rise and Fall of the Oslo Peace Process' in Fawcett, L. (ed.) *International Relations of the Middle East*, Oxford University Press, pp. 241–61.

—— (2007) *Lion of Jordan: The Life of King Hussein in War and Peace*, Penguin.

Smadi, M. (1998) 'Follow-up Report on the Trade and Economic Cooperation Agreement between Jordan and Israel', Peace Follow-up Unit, RSS–UNDP.

Spears, L. C. (ed.) (2000) 'The Power Servant Leadership', Foreword by Peter B. Vail,

UN University/ International Leadership Academy, course manual, Leadership in Post-conflict Peacebuilding.

Steinberg, G. (2002) 'Unripeness and Conflict Management: Re-examining the Oslo Process and its Lessons', Bar Ilan University, Israel, Occasional paper no. 4, 18 June.

Susser, A. (1994) *On Both Banks of the Jordan: A Political Biography of Wasfi al-Tal*, London: Cass.

——— (2000) *Jordan, Case Study of a Pivotal State*, The Washington Institute for Near East Policy.

Susser, A. and Shmuelevitz, A. (eds) (1995) *The Hashemites in the Modern Arab World*, Frank Cass & Co. Ltd.

Sussman, G. (2005) 'Ariel Sharon and the Jordan Option', *Middle East Report Online*, March. Available at www.merip.org/mero/interventions/sussman_interv.html.

Terry, D. J. and Hogg, M.A. (eds) (2000) *Attitudes, Behavior, And Social Context, The Role of Norms and Group Membership*, Lawrence Erlbaum Associates.

Thompson, E. (2000) 'Leadership in South Africa: How long does a rainbow last?', UNU/ International Leadership Academy, Alumni paper Series : paper no. 1.

UN Economic Survey Mission (September 1949) 'First Interim Report of UN Survey Mission for Middle East' (UN Document A/1106) finalized in November 1949.

United States Institute of Peace (2002) Special Report 82: 'Islamic Perspectives on Peace and Violence', January.

University of Science and Technology, Faculty of Arts and Humanities, Course: History of Jerusalem no. 1321

Väyrynen, R. (ed.) (1991) *New Directions in Conflict Theory: Conflict Resolution and Conflict Transformation*, Sage Publications.

Volker, P. (ed.) (2004) *Arab Elites: Negotiating the Politics of Change*, Lynne Rienner.

Wallensteen, P. (2004) *Understanding Conflict Resolution: War, Peace and the Global System*, Sage Publications.

Wendt, A. (1991) 'Bridging the Theory/Meta-theory Gap in International Relations', *Review of International Studies* 17(4): 383–92.

Williams, G. R. (1993) *Style and Effectiveness in Negotiation*, Sage Publications Inc.

Winter, M. (1995) 'The Arab Self-image as Reflected in Jordanian Textbooks', in Susser, A. and Shmuelevits, A. (eds) *The Hashemites in the Modern Arab World*, Frank Cass & Co. Ltd, pp. 207–20.

World Bank (1994) 'Peace and the Jordanian Economy', The International Bank for Reconstruction and Development.

Wren, T. J. and Swatez M. J. (2000) 'The Historical and Contemporary Contexts of Leadership', Chapter 36: Contexts of Leadership: A conceptual Model, UNU/ILA course manual, Leadership in Post-conflict Peacebuilding.

Index

Abbas, Mahmoud (Prime Minister,
    Palestine) 49, 64
Abdul Hameed Shohan Foundation 65
Abdullah I, King (Jordan) 9, 10
Abdullah II, King (Jordan) 29, 42, 76–7
Act of Union 1950 9
al-Fayez, Faisal (Prime Minister, Jordan) 64
al-Jazeera 39
al-Karama 13
Allon Plan 13–14
Allon, Yigal (Deputy Prime Minister,
    Israel) 14
Aloni, Shulamit (Meretz Party, Israel) 27
Amir, Yigal 32–3
anti-normalization movement 63–5, 78,
    93n26
Arab League: Summit 1964 10; Summit
    1982 14; Summit 1987 16; Summit
    1988 17
Arafat, Yasser: addresses UN European
    HQ 23–4; anti-imperialism 26; besieged
    42; calls for negotiations with Israel
    19–20; confined to Ramallah 54; elected
    chairman PLO executive committee 13;
    elected President Palestinian National
    Authority 50; Israeli elections 1999 40;
    makes agreement with Jordan 14; Oslo
    II Accords signed 50; signs Hebron
    Protocol 36; as terrorist 86
Arava Valley: peace treaty signed 1
autonomy: West Bank 12
Avineri, Professor Shlomo: substitute
    homeland 70
Ayyash, Yahya (Hamas): assassinated 34
Azar, E.: peacebuilding 5

Bank for Economic Cooperation and
    Reconstruction in the Middle East and
    North Africa: founded 32
Barak, Ehud (Prime Minister, Israel):
    elected 39; refuses to meet Yasser Arafat
    40–1; separation 71–2
Bassiouny, Salah: Israeli elections 1999 39
Beinin, Professor Joel: settlement building
    70
Ben-Gurion, David: lack of commitment
    9–10; rejects peace offer 23
Beres, Louis René: PNA (Palestinian
    National Authority) 52
bilateral cooperation: Jordan and Israel 31
bilateral relations: anti-normalization
    movement 65; Israel and Palestine 42,
    49; Jordan and Israel 33, 43, 49
Blair, Tony (Prime Minister, Great
    Britain): Roadmap 42–3
border crossings: trade 44
borders: demarcated 31; obstacles 20
Boutros Ghali, Boutros: peacebuilding 5
Bush, George W. (President, US): elected 42
business links with Israel: boycotts 78

Camp David 14, 28; summit collapses 41
Centre for Strategic Studies (Jordan
    University): public poll 3
Clinton, President Bill (US): Clinton
    Parameters 42; endorses peace process 21
confidence-building measures: expulsion
    of Hamas from Jordan 76; Israeli
    elections 1999 39; joint working 19;
    warm peace 74
conflict: linear views 7
conflict resolution: dominant perceptions
    22–8; emergence as a field of study 6–7
conflict transformation: structures 8;
    theory 7
cooperation: Jordan–Palestine 15

corruption: Jordanian government 78
culture: bilateral relations 65; structural
    role 8

Dadonn, David (Israeli Ambassador to
    Jordan): meets Dr Marwen Muasher 42
Dayan, Moshe: partition plan 14
Declaration Of Principles 18–19
Declaration of Principles (1993) 8
development: and peace 5
diplomatic relations: Jordan and Israel 31
disarmament: militant groups 52–3
displaced persons: defined 68

East Jerusalem: taken by Israel 11
economic cooperation: Jordan and Israel
    43–7
Egypt: land for peace 11; peace treaty with
    Israel 1, 14; Qualified Industrial Zones
    (QIZ) 46; United Arab Kingdom 13
Eshkol, Levi (Prime Minister, Israel):
    Palestinian refugees 27; threatened Arab
    nations 10–11

Fahd, King (Saudi Arabia): calls for peace
    86–7
Fatah: guerrilla activities 13; Intifada
    (2000) 41; violence 50
Fedayin attacks: against Israel 13
federation: Jordan and Palestine 13
Force 17: guerrilla attacks 15
foreign debt: Jordan 79
foreign investment: inefficient bureaucracy
    78; Qualified Industrial Zones (QIZ) 46
Free Trade Agreement (FTA): US-Jordan 46
Free Zones: Jordan 46–7
Frost, Robert: separation 71–2

Galtung, John: peacebuilding 4, 5, 89n1
Gaza: violence 36
Grapes of Wrath: Lebanon 34–5

Hamas: attacks Jerusalem 50; car bombs
    39; competition against PLO 51;
    founded 90n10; offices in Jordan closed
    29, 76; retaliation attacks 34; threat to
    PLO 7; violence 50
Hashemite Kingdom of Jordan: armistice
    with Israel 9; heritage 28
Hasmonean Tunnel: opened 36
Haugerudbraaten, H.: peacebuilding 5
Hebron Protocol: signed 36

Holocaust Syndrome: fed by Pan-Arab
    rhetoric 25
Hussein, King of Jordan: accedes to the
    throne 10; breaks ties with PLO 15;
    breaks ties with West Bank 17–18;
    confidence-building measures 36;
    ideological beliefs 28–9; Israeli public
    approval 74; London Agreement 16;
    peace treaty with Israel 21–2, 32; peace
    with Israel 3; peacebuilding 38, 87;
    popularity in Jordan 76; Rabin, Yitzhak
    31, 75; rejects Dayan Plan 14; Sharm El
    Sheikh 34; United Arab Kingdom 13;
    vision for peace 73–6; War of 1967 11

International Crisis Group: Palestinian
    refugees 27
international relations: conflict resolution 6
Intifada (1987): Israel 24; Jordan 18; lack
    of support for King Hussein 29; power
    balance 7; spontaneous 16–17
Intifada (2000): anti-normalization
    movement 65–6, 85; bilateral relations
    49; lack of support 79–80; led by Fatah
    41; provides status 55
Iran: threatened by Israel 34
Iraq: war 2003 84, 87
Islamic Action Front (Jordan): ideological
    beliefs 29–30
Islamic Jihad: competition against PLO 51;
    violence 50
Islamism: growth 25–6
Islamists: opposed to peace 62
Israel: backed by United States 7; bilateral
    relations with Jordan 33, 37, 43; called
    for Yasser Arafat to step down 54; closed
    economy 45; deals direct with PLO 18;
    dominance over Jordan 6; economic
    cooperation 43–7; elections 1999 39–40;
    fear of genocide 24; foreign policy
    22, 74–5; Intifada (2000) 80; military
    cooperation with Turkey 34; military
    victories 23; national interests 38;
    nuclear power 10; Palestinian incursions
    43; peace negotiations 3, 85; polarization
    50–1; retaliation against PLO 15;
    retaliation attacks 50, 56; retaliation
    policies 22, 24–5; right of return 69;
    suspicious of Arabs 23; suspicious of
    King Hussein 17; talks with *Waqf* 34;
    unilateral withdrawal 55; War of 1967
    11–12; warm peace 79

Israeli trade fair: anti-normalization movement 63

Jabotinsky Ze'ev: influence on Binyamin Netanyahu 35–6; nationalism 23
Jerusalem: Israeli sovereignty 36; partitioned 19; settlement building 36–7; share sovereignty 87; sovereignty 38
Jihad, Abu (Khalil Al Wazir): expelled from Jordan 15
Johnston Plan (1955): water rights 21
Jordan *see also* Hashemite Kingdom of Jordan: 1948-9 war 9; anti-normalization movement 62; bilateral relations with Israel 33, 37, 43; bilateral relations with Saudi Arabia 32; business links with Israel 56–7; consolidating peace with Israel 47; corruption 78; de facto peace with Israel 10; debt reduction 20, 58–9; economic cooperation 43–7; economic difficulty 17–18; economic growth 57; evaluation of peace process 84; exploitation 80; exports to Occupied territories 34; exports to US 47; financial aid 29; Hussein, King of Jordan 75; investment 59–60, 77; land for peace 11; middle-level leadership 79–81; Palestinian refugees 2, 4, 22, 27, 68, 69–70; Palestinian state 85; peace treaty with Israel 34; peace with Israel 75; Qualified Industrial Zones (QIZ) 45–7; refugee camps 6; regime stability 10; seeks peace with Israel 19; sense of betrayal 75–6; severs links with West Bank 29; sovereignty 20, 28, 70; substitute homeland threat 3, 27–8, 43, 83; threatened by Israel 84–5; unemployment 59; vision for peace 81; wants peace 8; War of 1967 11; warm peace 79
Jordan River: diverted 10
Jordan Times: Lebanon 56
Jordanian-Israeli conflict: asymmetry 5–6
Judea: biblical Jewish land 33

Kabarati, Abdul Karim (Prime Minister, Jordan): visits Israel 34
Al-Khazendar, S. 73
Kissinger, Henry 14–15

Labour Party (Israel) 33, 51
land for peace 53–4

Larsen, Terje Roed (United Nations) 71
Law of Return (Israel, 1950) 30
Lebanon 27, 34
Lederach, J.P. 5
Leftists 62
Likud government 14
Likud Party (Israel) 33, 51
Lustick, Ian S. 80

Madrid Peace Conference 8
Majali, Abdul Salam (Prime Minister, Jordan) 22, 28
Mandate line (1922) 20
Mashal, Khalid (Chief of Hamas Political Bureau, Jordan) 37
Meir, Golda (Prime Minister, Israel) 27
Middle East and North Africa Summit 1995 (MENA) 31–2, 56–7, 65
Morris, Benny 86
Mossad 37
Muasher, Dr Marwan (Deputy Prime Minister, Jordan) 72
Muasher, Dr Marwan (Foreign Minister, Jordan) 42
Mubarak, Hosni (President, Egypt) 36
Murad, Mahmoud 39
Musa, Amr (Foreign Minister, Egypt) 32, 34

Nasser, Gamal Abdel: defeated in War of 1967 11; hero to Palestinians 17; leadership attacked 10; Pan-Arab nationalism 26; resigns 25
National Religious Party (Israel) 14
nationalism 2, 12, 78–9
Navon, Benjamin 60
Netanyahu, Binyamin (Prime Minister, Israel): bilateral relations 49; credibility 39; elected 35–6, 50; Jordanian sovereignty 74; Mossad assassination attempt 37; settlement building 38–9, 51; signs Hebron Protocol 36; substitute homeland 71
normalization: Abdullah II, King (Jordan) 76; anti-normalization movement 74; anti-normalization movement in Jordan 60–1; disagreement 32; Egypt and Israel 1; exploitation 61; hindered 66; Hussein, King of Jordan 74; inefficient bureaucracy 77; Islamic opposition 29–30; lack of structural change 84; Palestinian refugees 4; Palestinian state 79; support 76

Occupied Territories: Intifada (2000) 80;
Israel 17; living standards 54–5; militant
groups 55; Nasser, Gamal Abdel 25;
native residents 68; Qualified Industrial
Zones (QIZ) 46; sealed by Israel 50;
settlement building 16; unemployment
55; unilateral withdrawal 71; uprising 7;
violence 49–51
October 1973 war 14
Oslo Accords 18, 36, 50, 54–5, 67, 90n11

Palestine 23
Palestinian National Charter 18
Palestinian refugees: 1948 war 89n3;
camp dwellers 55–6; citizenship 68;
defined 68; economic hardships 41–2;
given Jordanian citizenship 10, 15;
identity 26; Israeli denial 27; Jordan
67; Jordanian peace with Israel 3; peace
process 2; radicalized 67; right of return
53, 68–9
peace 4
peace treaty with Israel 1, 21
peacebuilding: defined 4–5; deterioration
83–4; formal peace 74; Israel-
Palestine 69; lack of commitment 54;
sustainability 7
Peres, Shimon: antagonized Arab world
35; authorized assassination of Yahya
Ayyash 34; Hamas 52; London
Agreement 16; New Middle East 62;
Oslo II Accords signed 50; succeeded
Yitzhak Rabin 33–4
PLO (Palestinian Liberation Organisation):
ambitions for peace 2; arrests of
Hamas members 53; betrays Jordan
75–6; corruption 16; creation 27;
establishment of a state 3; Fedayin
attacks 13; founded 10; guerrilla attacks
15; Hussein, King of Jordan 75; lack
of popularity 7; leadership confirmed
17; representation of Palestinians 28–9;
response to Hamas 52–6; right of return
69; substitute homeland 70; two-state
solution 18, 87; United Arab Kingdom
13; Washington Declaration 19
PNA (Palestinian National Authority):
Israeli elections 1999 39–40; peace
process 52; returnees 68; violence 38;
Yasser Arafat elected President 50
PNC (Palestinian National Council) 13, 24
polarization 33

positive peace 5, 7
power asymmetry 7, 83

Qaddumi, Farouq 53
Qualified Industrial Zones (QIZ):
competition 59; customs clearance
78; foreign workers 58; joint business
ventures 32, 57; Jordan 45–7

Rabin, Yitzhak: assassinated 32–3;
Hussein, King of Jordan 31, 75; meets
Abdul Karim Kabarati 34–5; Oslo II
Accords signed 50; threatened Arab
nations 11
Rahman, As'ad Abdul (PLO Department
of Refugee Affairs) 67
Ramon, Haim (Labour Party, Israel) 72
refugees 21–2, 25
regime stability 11
Regional Business Council 59
Regional Business Council (RBC) 32
Regional Tourism Board 32
Rosati, J.A. 25

Salhi, Bassam (Palestinian People's Party)
27
Samaria 33
Samu village 10
Saudi Arabia 32
settlement building 33, 54, 70, 71
Shamir, Shimon 1
Shamir, Yitzhak (Prime Minister, Israel)
7, 16, 24
Sharm El Sheikh 34
Sharon, Ariel: builds wall 86; demands
retaliation 15; elected 42; meets
Mahmoud Abbas 49; Roadmap 43;
substitute homeland 70–1; visits Jordan 37
Shuqairi, Ahmad (Chairman, PLO) 70
Six Day War (1967) 10, 12
Soffer, Professor Arnon 85
sovereignty 12
standards 44–5, 77–8
state sovereignty 6
structures 7
substitute homeland 2, 22, 70–2, 79
Syria 11, 34, 36

tariffs 44
territorial claims 2
terrorism 24
tourism 60, 66

Trade and Economic Cooperation
  Agreement 43–7
trade relations 45, 57–8, 74, 77–8
two-state solution: Arafat, Yasser 53;
  not favoured by Palestinian militants
  50; Palestinian leadership 67; PLO
  (Palestinian Liberation Organisation) 7,
  16; right of return 69

UN Security Council: resolution 1397 54;
  resolution 1405 71; resolution 1420 54;
  resolution 181 23; resolution 242 12,
  17; resolution 338 14
unemployment 55, 57, 59
United States 14, 38, 79, 92n15
UNRWA (United Nations Relief and
  Works Agency) 69, 94n4

Väyrynen, R. 56
violence 6, 54, 55

warm peace 2, 83, 86
Washington Declaration 1, 3, 19, 20
water rights 2, 20, 33–4, 43; Jordan 89n2
al-Wazir, Khalil 15
Weizman, Exer 34–5
West Bank: annexed by Israel 11; annexed
  by Jordan 9; autonomy 50; economic
  links strengthened with Jordan 15;
  territorial claims 12; violence 36
World Economic Forum 2003 (WEF) 57

Yassin, Sheikh Ahmed 37, 43

Zaim, President Husni (Syria) 23
Zionism: confused with Judaism 30;
  nationalism 22–3; Palestinian refugees
  27; religious 33; Revisionist policies 35;
  War of 1967 12

For Product Safety Concerns and Information please contact our EU
representative GPSR@taylorandfrancis.com
Taylor & Francis Verlag GmbH, Kaufingerstraße 24, 80331 München, Germany